EROTIC ORIGAMI

Marc Kirschenbaum

Fit to Print Publishing, Inc.
New York, New York

Erotic Origami

Copyright © 2008, 2019
Fit To Print Publishing, Inc.

All rights reserved. No part of this publication may be reproduced, stored in a retrieval system or transmitted in any form or by any means, electronic, mechanical, photocopying, recording or otherwise, without the permission of the copyright holder.

Library of Congress Control Number: 2008903877

ISBN 978-1-951146-07-8 (Paperback Edition)
ISBN 978-1-951146-08-5 (Hardcover Edition)

The diagrams in this book were produced with Macromedia's Freehand, and image processing was done with Adobe Photoshop. The Backtalk family of typefaces was used for the body text and Playtoy was used for the cover. Ellen Cohen provided photography, layout and editing assistance; any remaining errors are the fault of the author.

Contents

Introduction	5
Symbols and Terminology	6
Anally Receptive	10
Ankh	14
Smoker	22
Lips Together, Teeth Apart	28
Mouney Fold	36
Prince Albert	42
Randy Rabbit	48
Taking a Hand in Female Matters	54
Taking a Hand in Male Matters	62
The Missionary	70
It's All Greek to Me	80
Each One Eat One	90
Materials and Methods	102
Ratio Information	111

Introduction

Virtually all art forms have explored erotic themes, and origami is no exception. Still, many people will be surprised to find how paperfolding artists can transform innocent sheets of paper into risqué forms. Origami is a relatively new art, so many people are not familiar with the boundaries that have been pushed for the past fifty years. I have found origami to be an ideal medium for expressing adult themes. While other art forms might border on being tasteless when depicting graphic material, the abstraction inherent in origami can play with the viewer's interpretation in unexpected ways. The stigma of showing a nude form in public seems to have been removed; yet the erotic underpinnings have not been distilled. On a technical level, expressing the human form, (and excerpts of the body) through origami has produced some interesting design challenges. These pieces fall into the advanced origami category. The diagrams are comprehensive after you become conversant with the notation utilized. The standard Yoshizawa-Randlett symbols are used, and there are many helpful hints in the instructions. A section on materials and methods is included, so you can emulate the look of each piece. Most importantly, this book is meant to be fun. You might never look at a piece of paper the same way again.

Symbols and Terminology

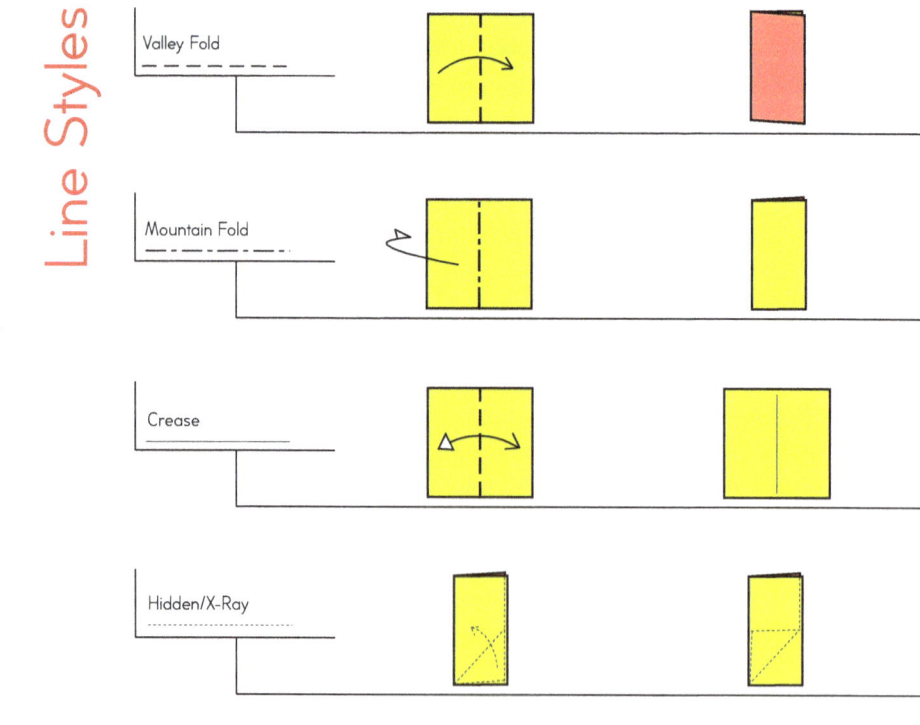

Arrows

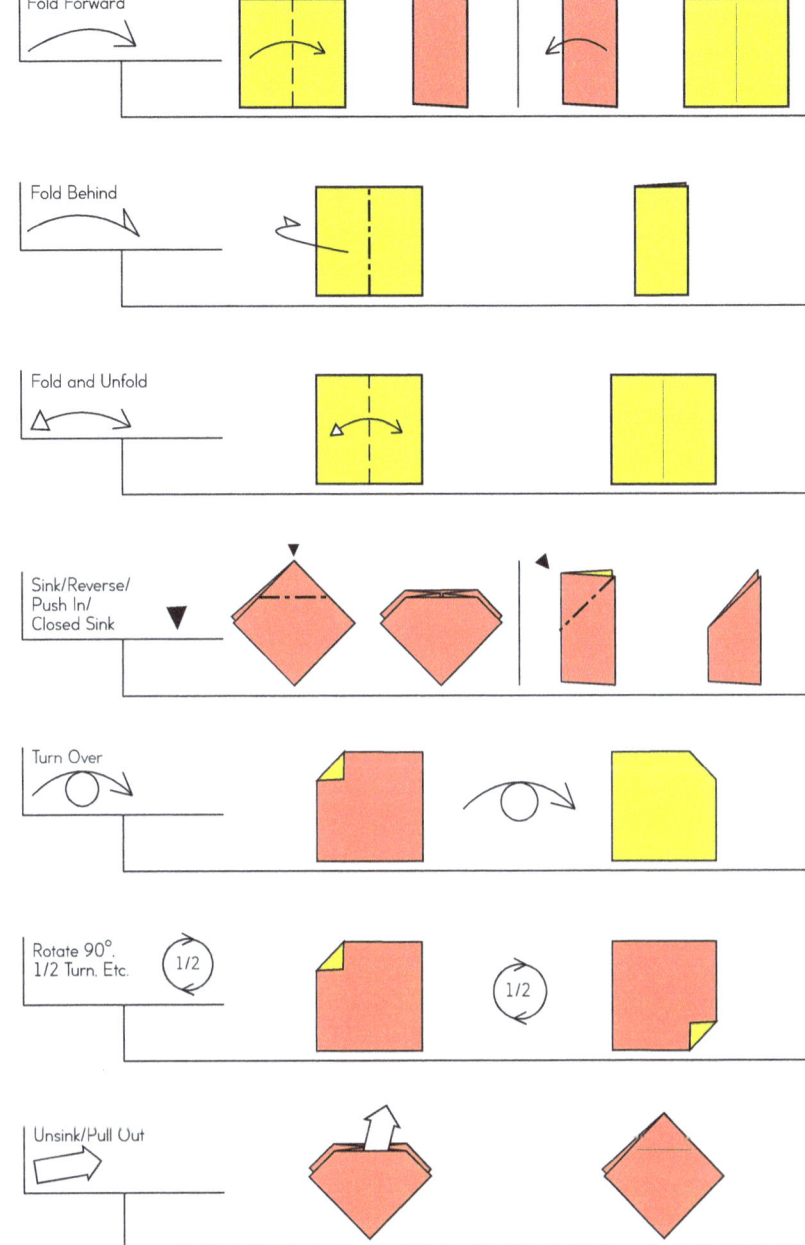

Maneuvers

- Reverse Fold
- Crimp
- Rabbit Ear
- Squash
- Petal Fold
- Sink
- Closed Sink

Sink Triangularly

Pleat

Swivel

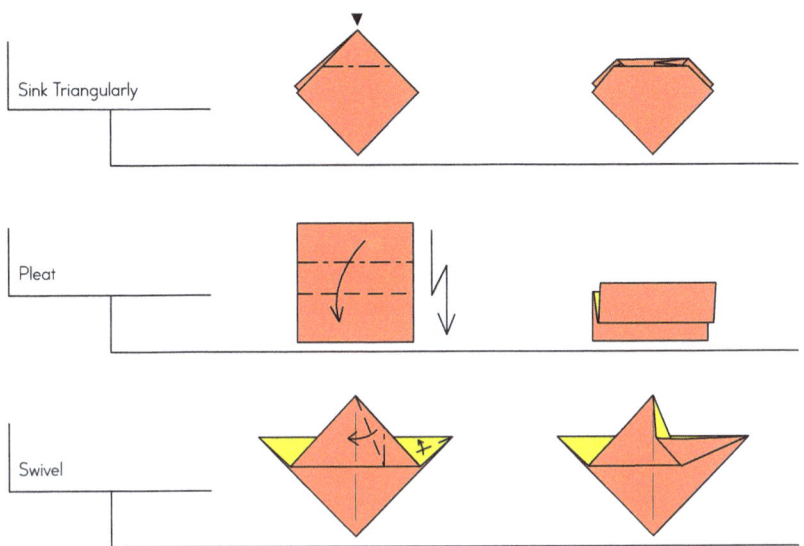

Anally Receptive

About

What origami design would be appropriate for an openly gay and flamboyant television host? *Anally Receptive* was designed and meant to be folded by the studio audience. As a model for the general public, it had to be quick and easy. Using the *Pureland* approach of folding (John Smith's term for an origami piece that uses only simple mountain and valley folds), a twelve-step model was devised. Formed alone it is simply a person in a bent-knee position, but it can be interconnected with additional folded instances of itself. Alas, an orgy of anally receptive modules was never fully realized, as *Anally Receptive* did not make it to the British television show. The joined-at-the-rear couple however, did show some life with some other British outlets. Nick Robinson, the charismatic origami artist from Sheffield, showcased the piece (uncredited) in his book *Adult Origami*. A variation on the piece, titled *Pureland Person*, won the British Origami Society President's Prize for the best simple design of a human figure. Time will tell how well the twosome will do in the States.

Tips

Since this piece only uses mountain and valley folds, it is an ideal warm up. Pay close attention to the reference points shown. Some intersections are marked with a dot for extra clarity. Once completed, connecting the people might prove to be a balancing act. Using paper that is somewhat rough will prevent the duo from sliding apart.

— anally receptive —

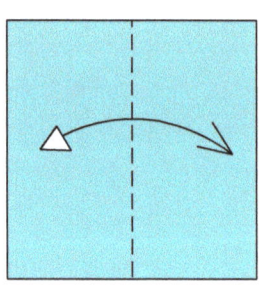

1. Precrease in half.

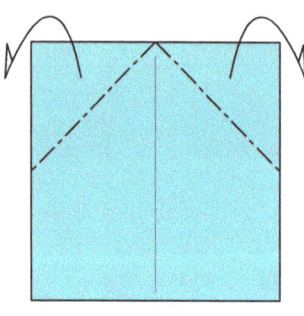

2. Mountain fold the top corners.

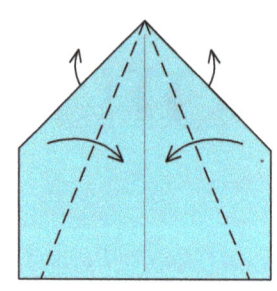

3. Valley fold the sides to the center, allowing the back flaps to flip outwards.

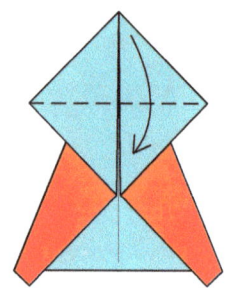

4. Valley fold down.

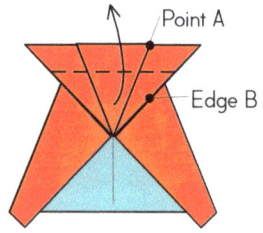

5. Valley fold the flap up, such that edge B hits point A.

6. Valley fold the tip of the flap down a bit.

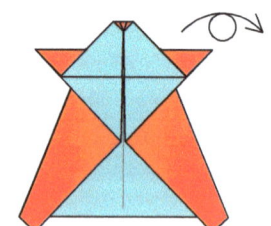

7. Turn over.

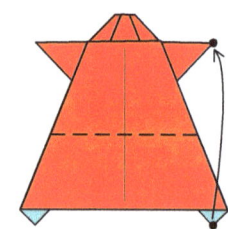

8. Valley fold up, allowing the indicated points to meet.

— anally receptive —

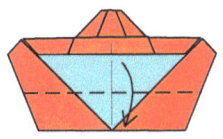 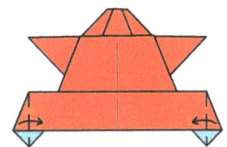 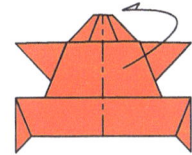 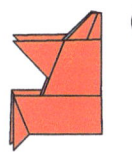

9. Valley fold the raw edge down to the bottom.

10. Valley fold the bottom tips in half.

11. Mountain fold the model in half.

12. Rotate the model, and make another (or more) for insertion.

13. Completed *Anally Receptive*.

Ankh

About

As with many misunderstood symbols, the ankh eventually took on a sexual connotation. The Egyptian hieroglyphic has a literal translation of "life," but has expanded to represent the power of reproduction. Its mystic appeal has popularized it, making the ankh a favorite image for tattoo artists. A certain famous, sexually-infused musician modified the symbol to represent himself for several years. When folded with striking colors (like gold and black) this ankh model will set a mood for the more overtly sexual pieces. Designing this model involved getting the raw edges of the starting square to lie along the interior area. Some flaps are inverted to reveal their contrasting color. Forming the interior edges at varying angles creates the illusion of curves. Part of the challenge was to come up with reference points that are reasonably easy to locate, without compromising too much of the artistic integrity.

Tips

Many of the folds use unusual reference points, so you will have to pay careful attention to the diagrams. Step thirty-two will be difficult if the idea of inverting a flap is new to you. Do one side at a time and unfold as much of the flap as you can in this step. Remember, you can always unfold the bottom flap completely and return to the position in step twenty-nine.

ankh

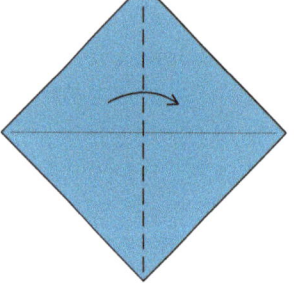

1. Precrease with a mountain fold.

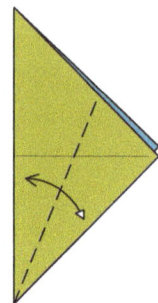

2. Valley fold in half.

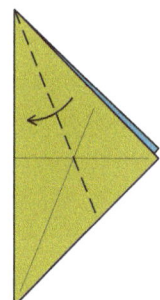

3. Precrease along the angle bisector.

4. Valley fold.

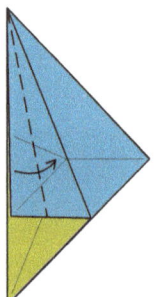

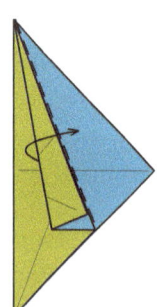

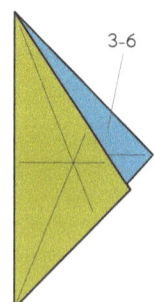

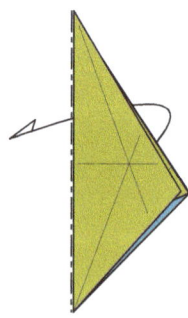

5. Valley fold along the angle bisector.

6. Swing over.

7. Repeat steps 3-6 behind.

8. Open out from along the center.

ankh

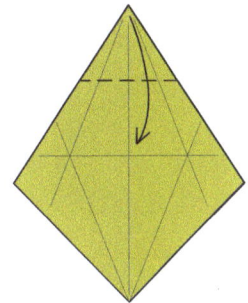 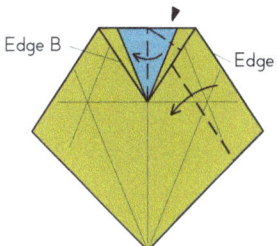 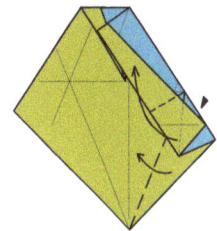 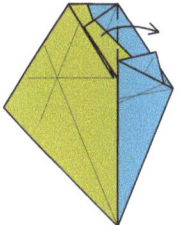

9. Valley fold to the intersection of creases.

10. Squash fold, such that edge A lies on edge B.

11. Squash upwards.

12. Valley fold over.

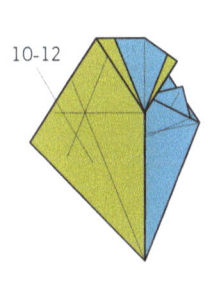 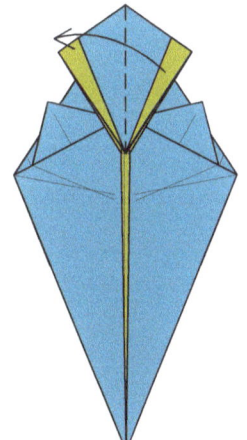 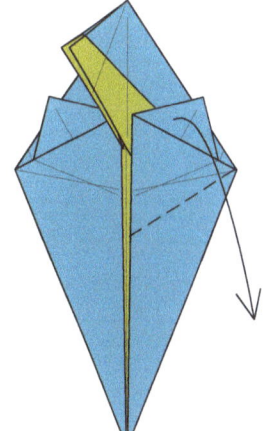 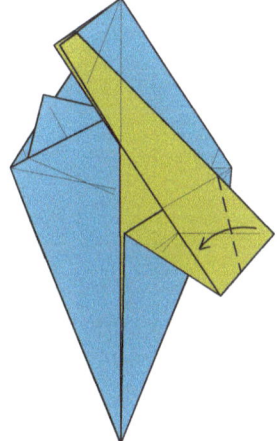

13. Repeat steps 10-12 in mirror image.

14. Swing over.

15. Valley fold down.

16. Valley fold the corner to the folded edge.

ankh

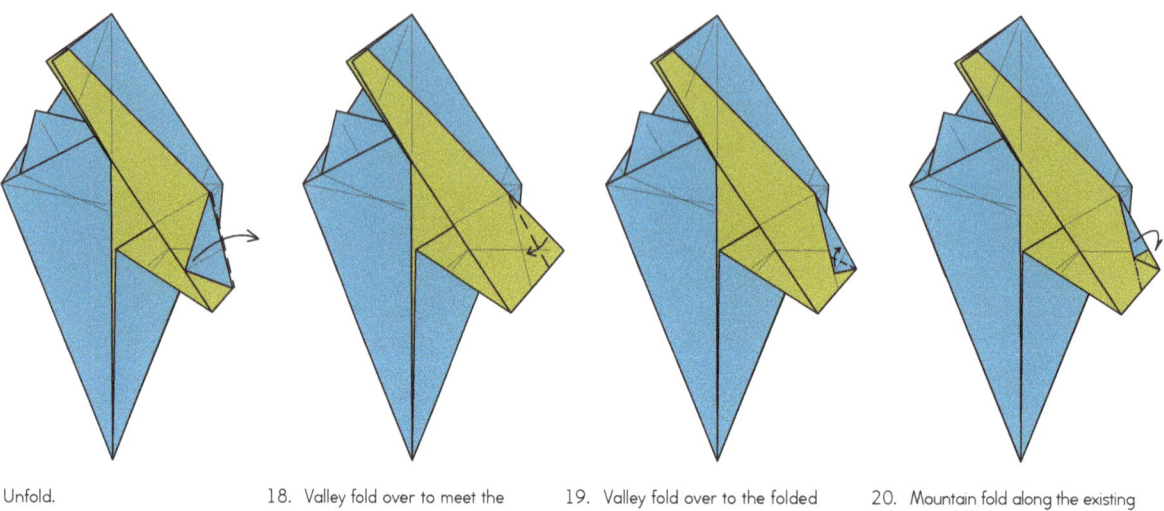

17. Unfold.

18. Valley fold over to meet the previous crease.

19. Valley fold over to the folded edge.

20. Mountain fold along the existing crease.

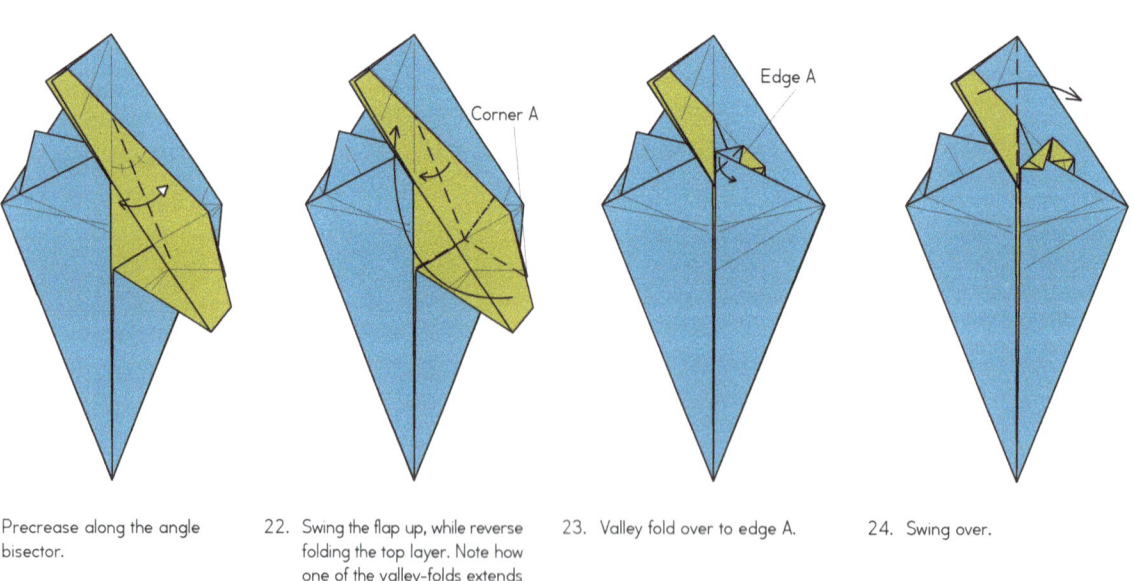

21. Precrease along the angle bisector.

22. Swing the flap up, while reverse folding the top layer. Note how one of the valley-folds extends from corner A.

23. Valley fold over to edge A.

24. Swing over.

— a n k h —

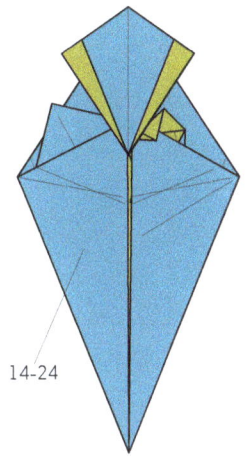

25. Repeat steps 14-24 in mirror image.

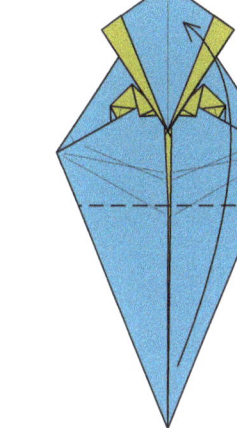

26. Valley fold to the top.

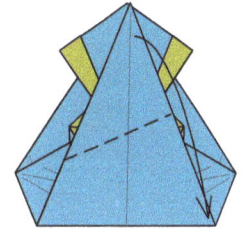

27. Valley fold to the corner.

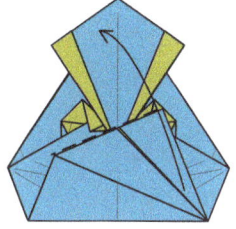

28. Unfold.

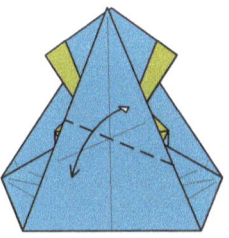

29. Repeat the precrease in the opposite direction.

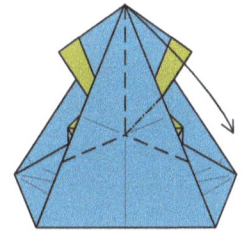

30. Rabbit ear.

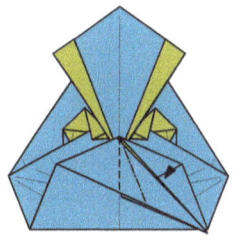

31. Squash fold.

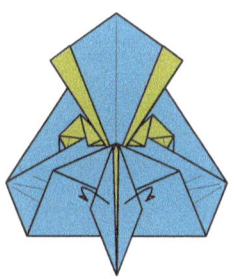

32. Wrap a single layer around each side.

ankh

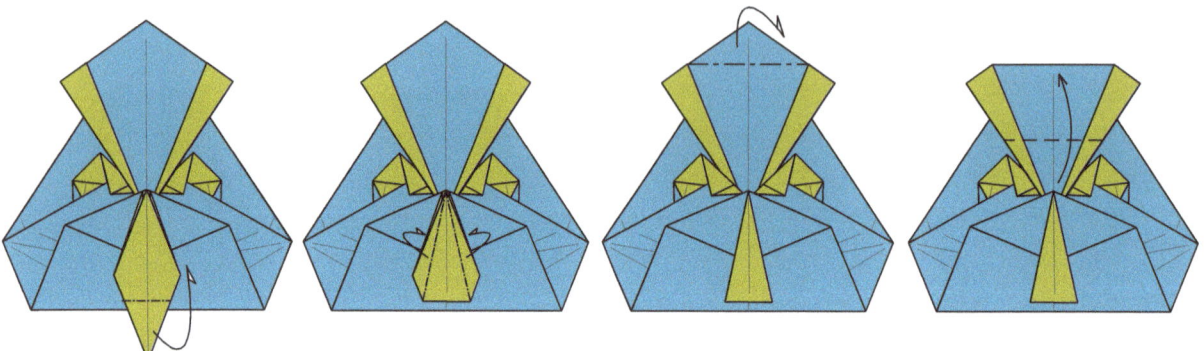

33. Mountain fold about 1/3rd the length of the flap.

34. Mountain fold the sides.

35. Mountain fold the top.

36. Lightly valley fold to the top.

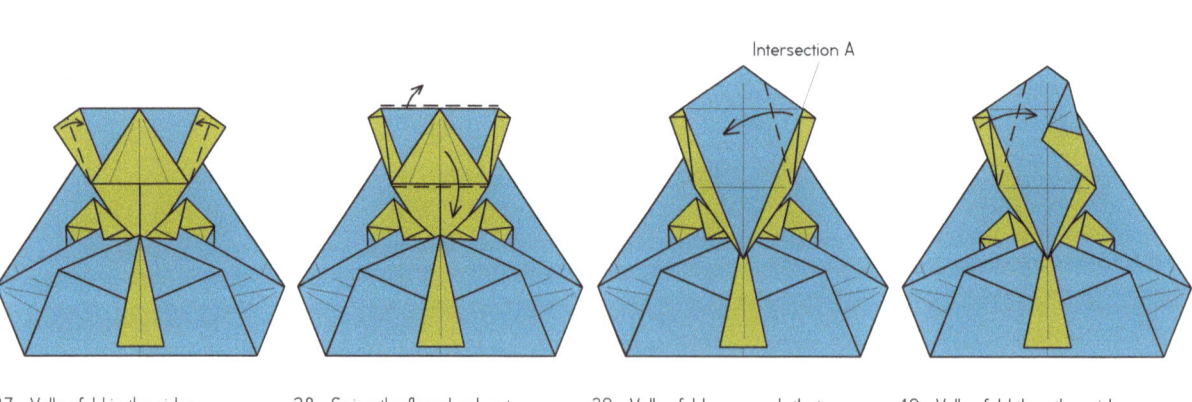

37. Valley fold in the sides.

38. Swing the flaps back out.

39. Valley fold over, such that intersection A lies along the center.

40. Valley fold the other side over to match.

ankh

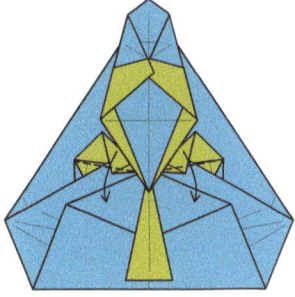

41. Valley fold down the two flaps. The folds extend from corner to corner.

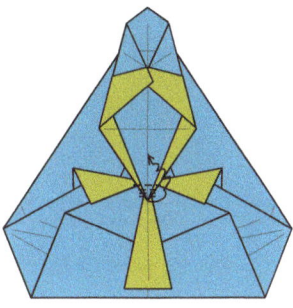

42. Valley fold the tip over and over to make it blunt.

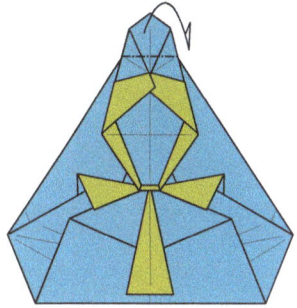

43. Mountain fold, using the existing crease as a guide.

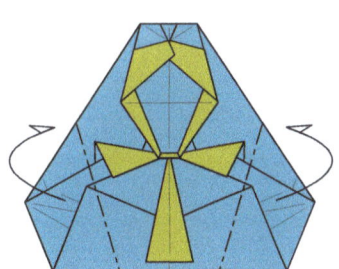

44. Mountain fold the sides to taste. If you leave the sides out at 90°, the model will stand.

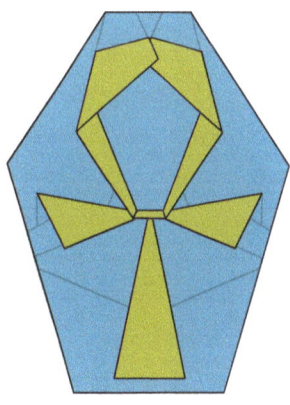

45. Completed *Ankh*.

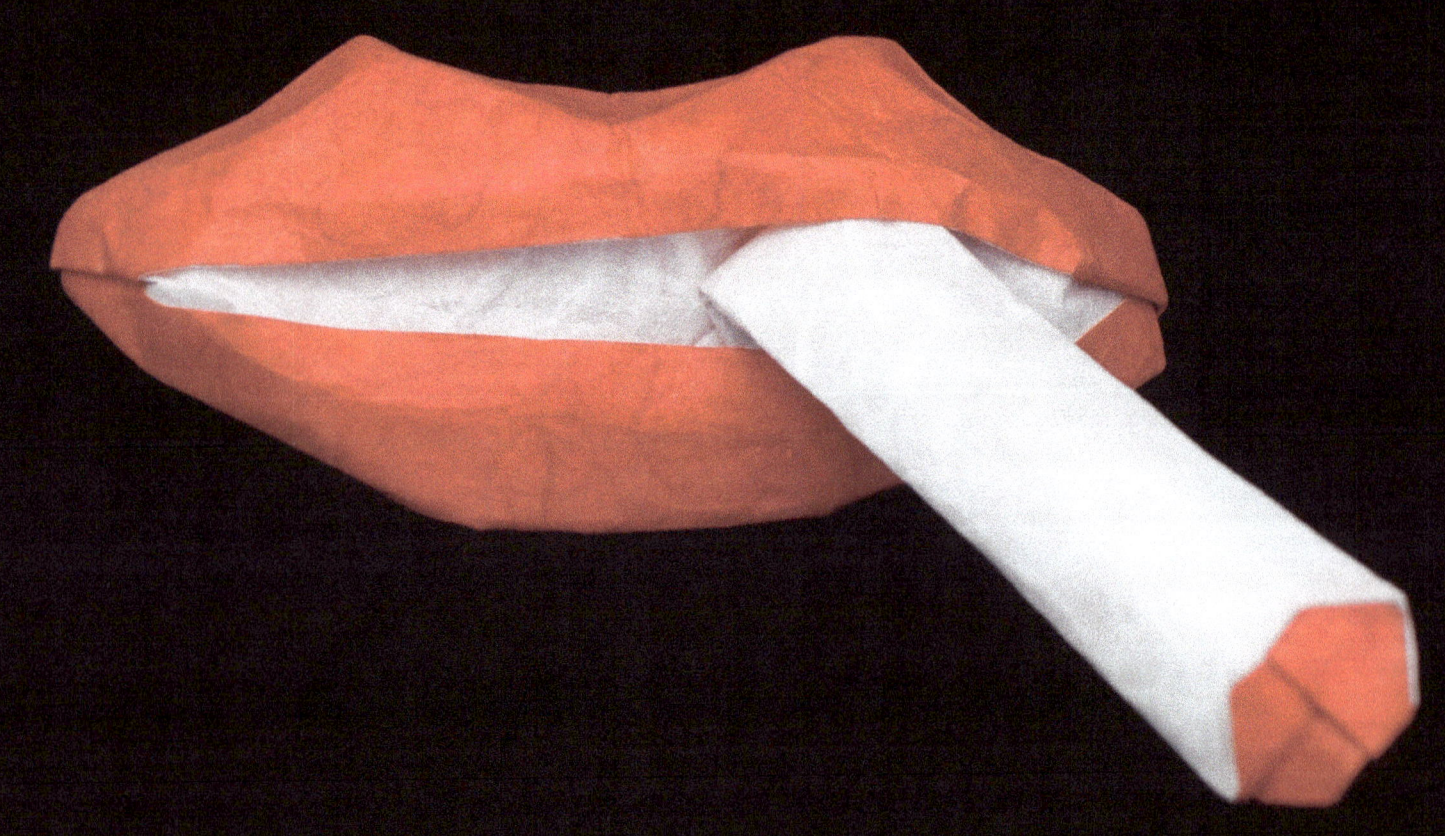

Smoker

About

This work is based on *Lips Together, Teeth Apart*, which showcases a more risqué adornment coming from the mouth. Changing the ratio of paper allocated for the lips creates the smaller appendage needed for the cigarette. Some people will regard anything dangling from the mouth as phallic, and the exaggerated lips in this piece make it more sexually suggestive. Though tobacco is known to be an unhealthy habit; this work simply regales in the old Hollywood technique of adding a cigarette to create a sexy appeal.

Tips

The first few steps are loosely based on the classic Bird Base, so those folds should be easy if you have ever made an origami crane. As with the Ankh, you will be inverting sections, but this time it will be difficult to unfold the model. If you feel a section of paper is under stress while inverting, be sure to grasp that section to prevent ripping. Forming the lips is an artistic challenge; most of the folds are easy but getting the lips to curve properly requires a good eye.

smoker

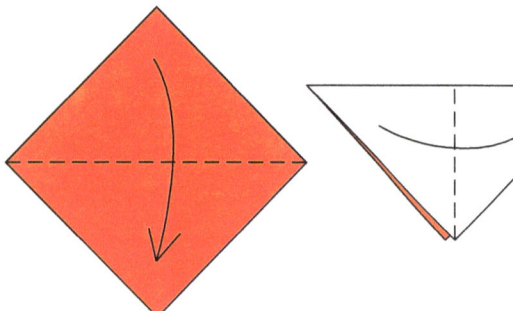

1. Valley fold in half.

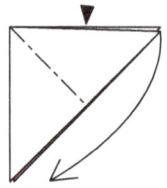

2. Valley fold in half.

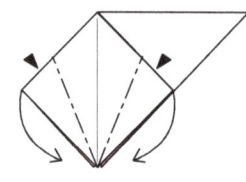

3. Squash fold.

4. Reverse fold the sides.

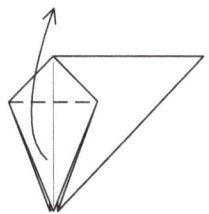

5. Valley fold the top flap up.

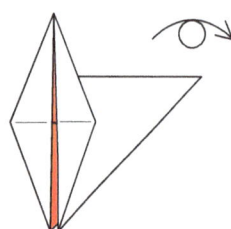

6. Turn over.

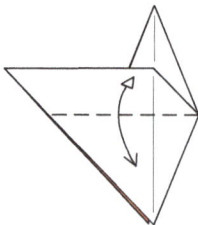

7. Precrease by swinging the middle section down and then up.

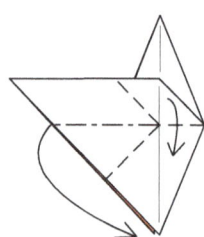

8. Bring the middle section down while reverse folding.

smoker

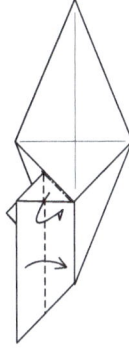

9. Valley fold the flap in half while swiveling under.

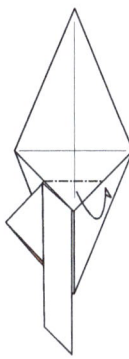

10. Swivel the flap under.

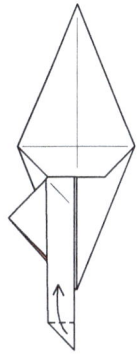

11. Valley fold the tip upwards.

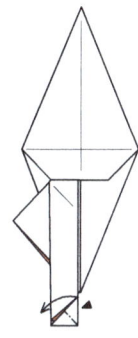

12. Squash fold.

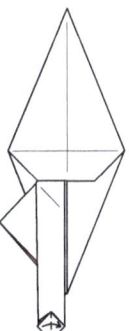

13. Valley fold the top single layer over.

14. Mountain fold the top and bottom corners slightly.

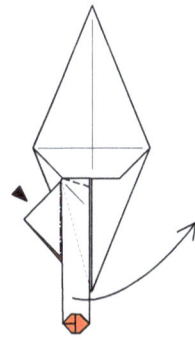

15. Squash fold the flap over.

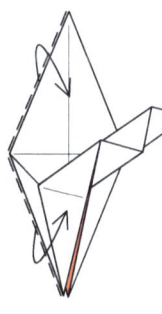

16. Wrap around a single layer from behind.

smoker

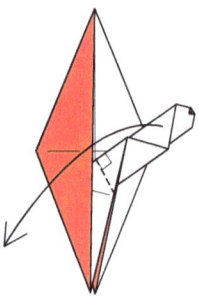

17. Valley fold the flap over.

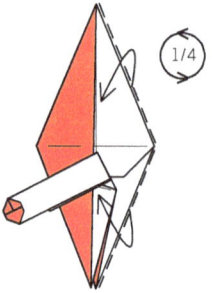

18. Wrap around a single layer from behind. Rotate the model 1/4 turn.

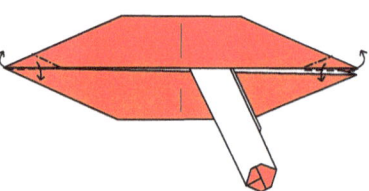

20. Crimp the corners of the lips, making them 3-D.

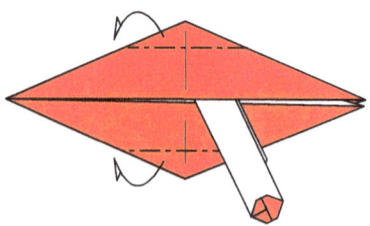

19. Shape with mountain folds.

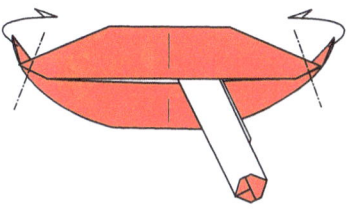

21. Mountain fold the corners to lock.

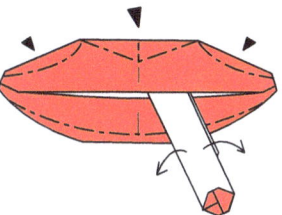

22. Shape the model to taste.

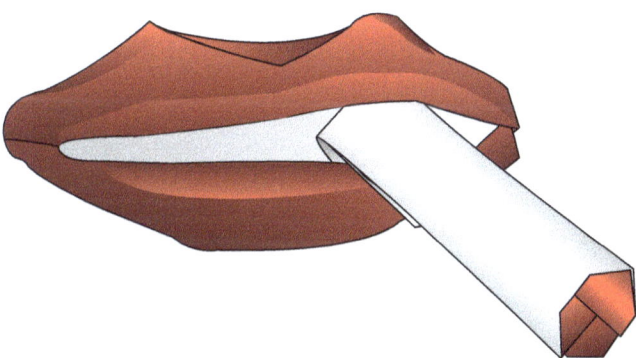

23. Completed *Smoker*.

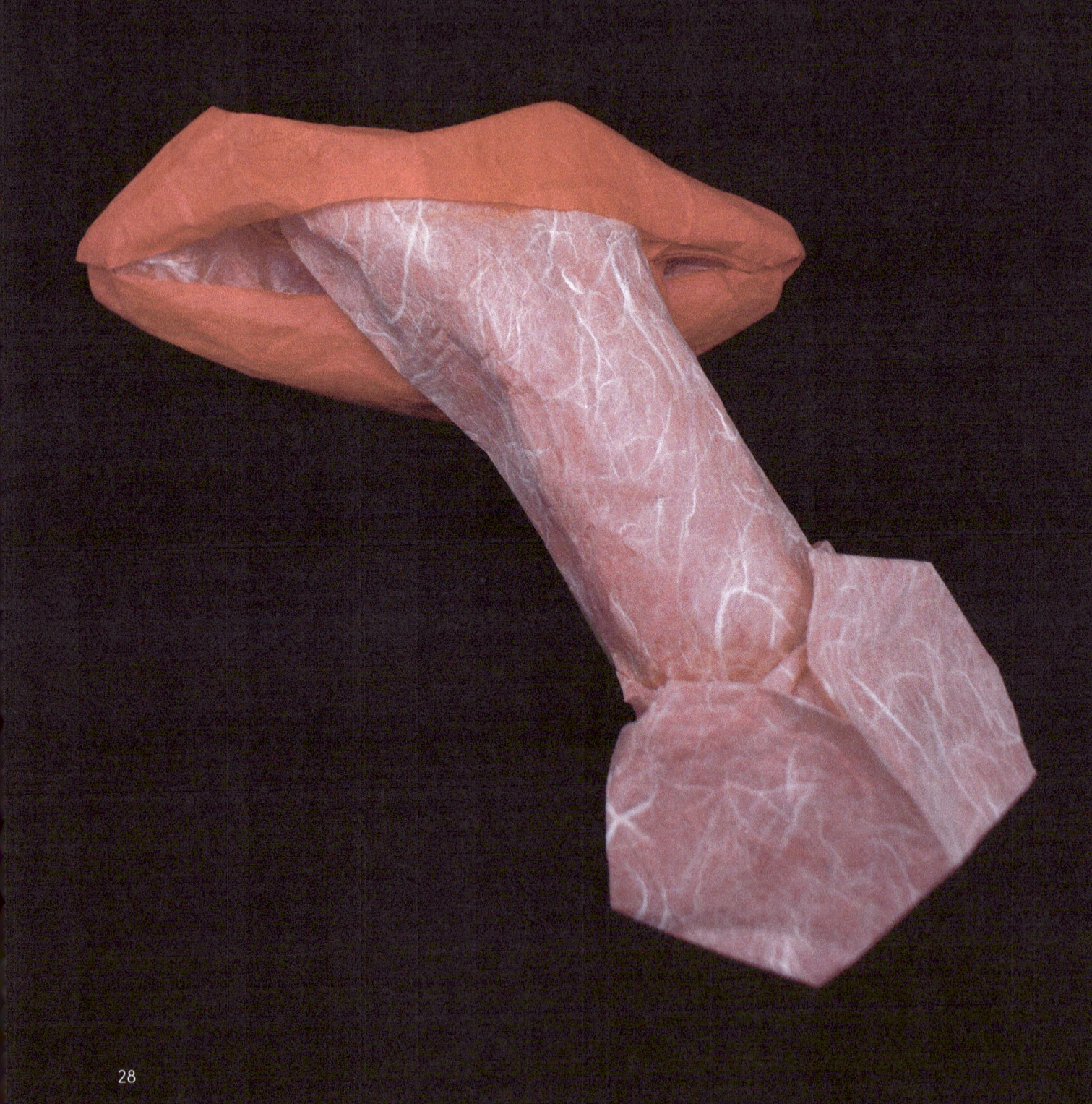

Lips Together, Teeth Apart

About

Many fellatio recipients prefer their partners to keep their *Lips Together, Teeth Apart*. Terrence McNally recognized this preference when he introduced the phase as a title for one for his plays. Incongruous to the crude subject matter, there are some sophisticated design elements. The reference point from step four has been independently discovered by some of the top origami designers and makes for an interesting starting point. The flap for the penis is structurally asymmetrical, making the extraction of a scrotum that much more satisfying. The penis is a bit large relative to the surrounding lips, but a more pedestrian-sized member would not have the same impact.

Tips

Some of the folds in this model (like step forty) are hidden from view, adding an extra challenge. Still, the flap can be opened from the side, enabling easy access. As with the *Smoker* piece, the lips will be an artistic challenge.

— lips together, teeth apart —

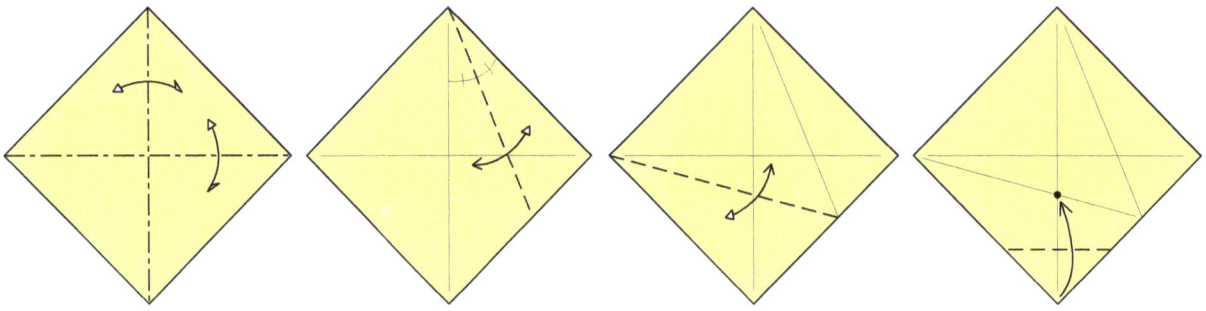

1. Precrease in half with mountain folds, both horizontally and vertically.

2. Precrease along the angle bisector.

3. Precrease, joining the end of the last crease to the corner.

4. Valley fold to the indicated intersection.

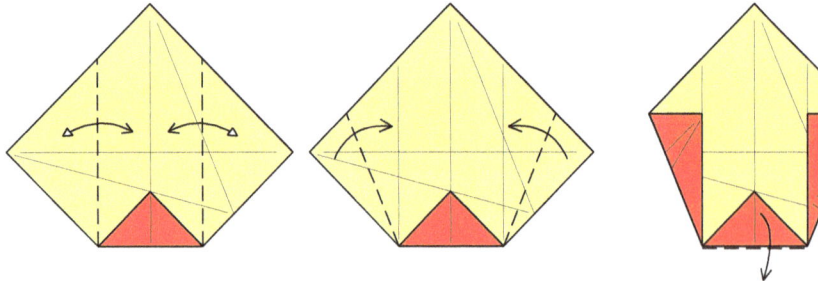
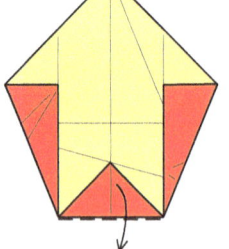
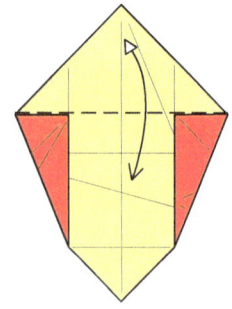

5. Precrease the sides.

6. Valley fold the sides to the creases.

7. Unfold the bottom flap.

8. Precrease the top.

lips together, teeth apart

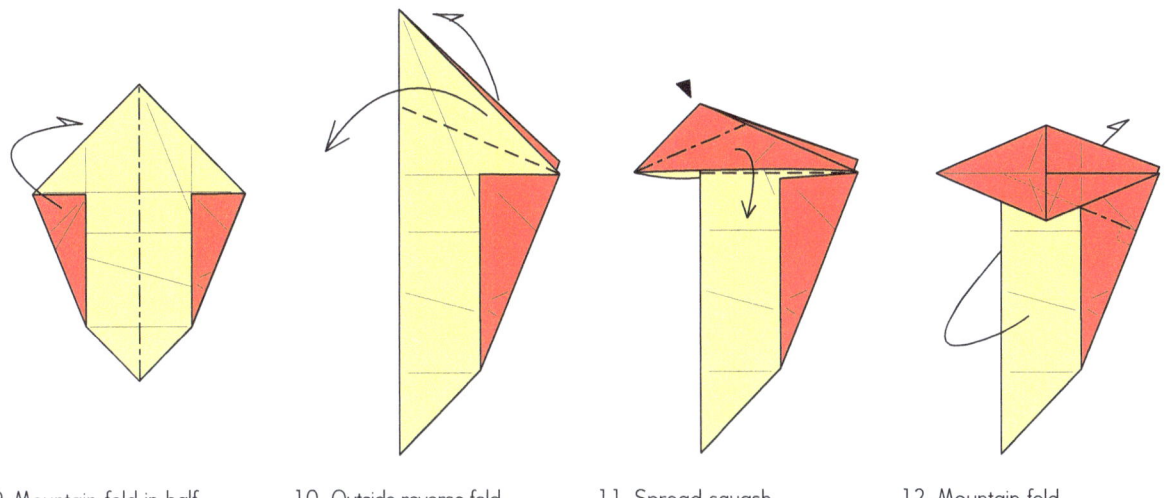

9. Mountain fold in half.

10. Outside reverse fold.

11. Spread squash.

12. Mountain fold.

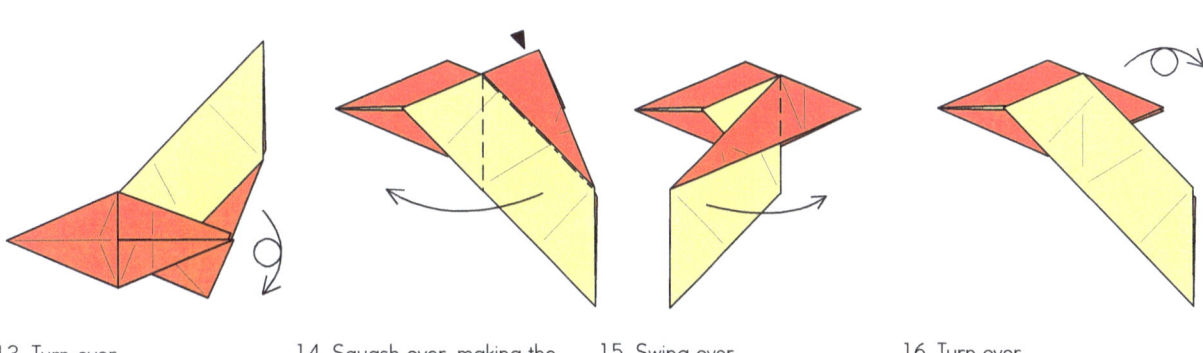

13. Turn over.

14. Squash over, making the valley fold as light as possible.

15. Swing over.

16. Turn over.

31

lips together, teeth apart

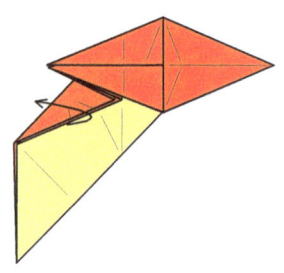

17. Wrap around a layer.

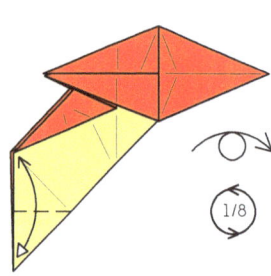

18. Precrease. Turn over and rotate.

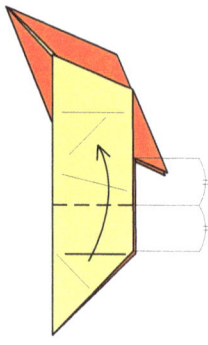

19. Valley up.

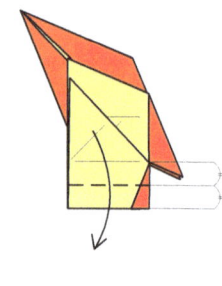

20. Valley down.

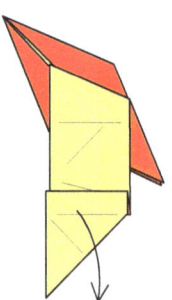

21. Undo the pleat.

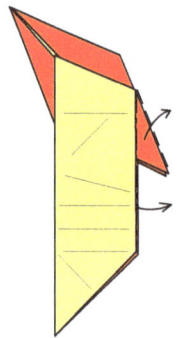

22. Pull out one layer.

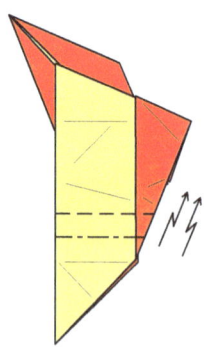

23. Crimp along the existing creases.

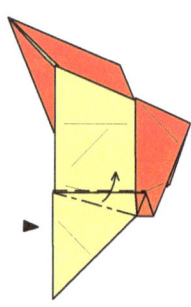

24. Lightly squash upwards. Do not flatten.

lips together, teeth apart

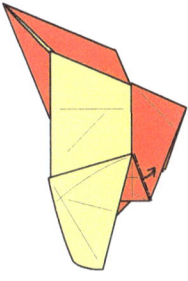 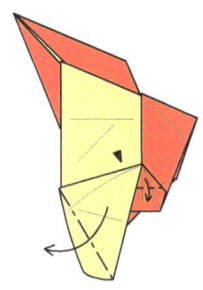 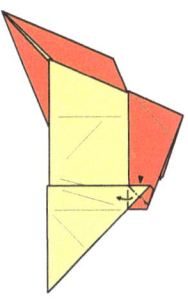 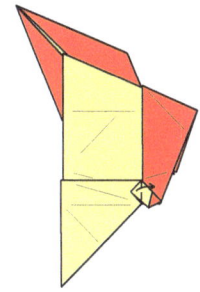

25. Slide out the single layer to match the right edge.
26. Squash back down.
27. Form a small squash.
28. Swing over.

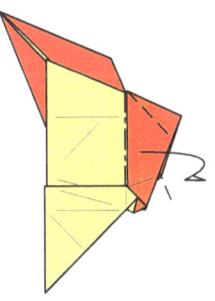 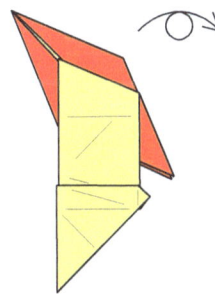 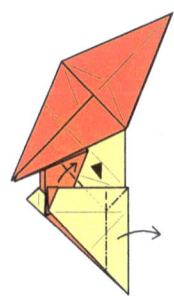 

29. Reverse the colored section back in.
30. Turn over.
31. Squash into a 3-D shape.
32. Squash flat.

33

— lips together, teeth apart —

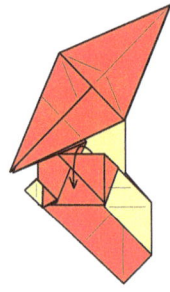

33. Wrap round one layer.

34. Swing one flap up.

35. Swivel up.

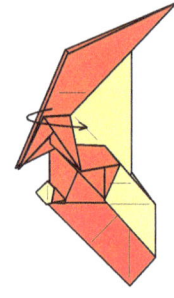

36. Pull two layers around the flap.

37. Swing back down.

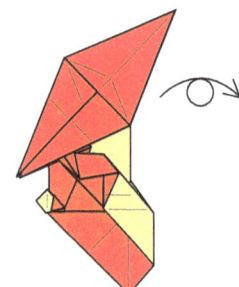

38. Turn over.

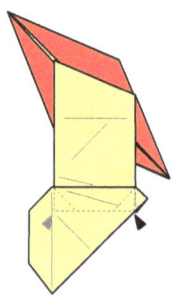

39. Reverse fold the hidden corners.

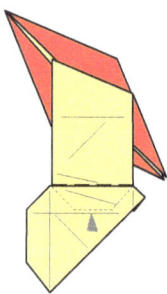

40. Closed sink the hidden flap through.

lips together, teeth apart

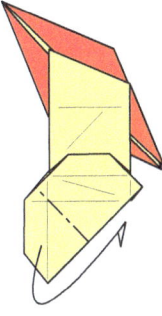 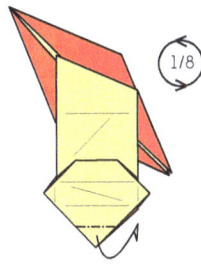 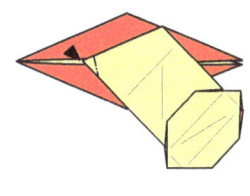 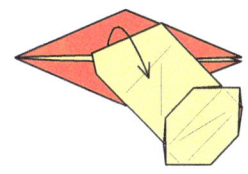

41. Mountain fold along the existing crease, tucking under the back flap to lock.

42. Mountain fold. Rotate the model slightly.

43. Open sink the corner. You will have to open out the model to do this.

44. Wrap around the single layer.

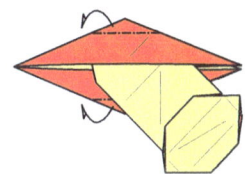 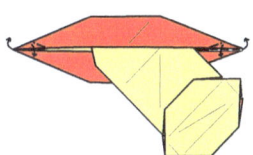 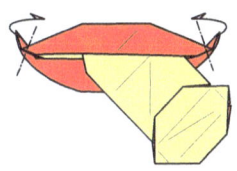 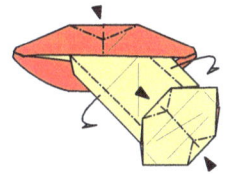

45. Shape with mountain folds.

46. Crimp the corners of the lips, making them 3-D.

47. Mountain fold the corners to lock.

48. Shape the model to taste.

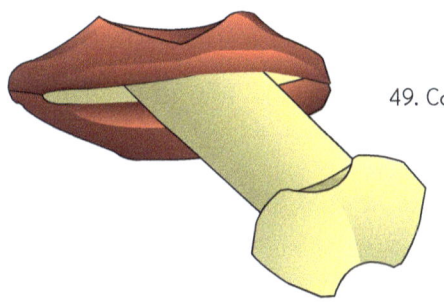

49. Completed *Lips Together, Teeth Apart*.

Mouney Fold

About

The American dollar has reigned as one of the most popular folding mediums. Here in the United States, origami artists will always be ready for an impromptu folding request with their on hand legal tender. The sheer novelty of turning something commonplace into art is certainly an attraction to the material. Still, you must wonder if there is a hidden meaning with such an iconic material choice. Does forming a vagina from a dollar have any reflection on its worth? As with most art, such answers are left to the observer. The mystery of the "Mouney" spelling can be revealed, however. In Yiddish, it is one of the many terms for the female privates. On a side note, "knish" is another Jewish word for vagina (perhaps explaining why they are often mated with wieners), but it is not phonetically like any form of currency.

Tips

For your first attempt, using a crisp dollar will help placing the folds more accurately. Once familiar with the sequence, a slightly worn bill will give the softness necessary to make the piece more effective. You will also soon discover that the accurate placement of the later folds is not so critical; a little sloppiness adds to the realism.

— mouney fold —

1. Begin with a dollar bill, "ONE" side up. Precrease along the diagonals.

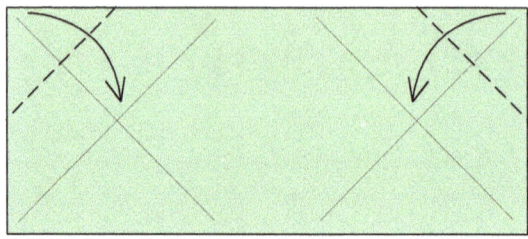

2. Valley fold the corners to the intersections of creases.

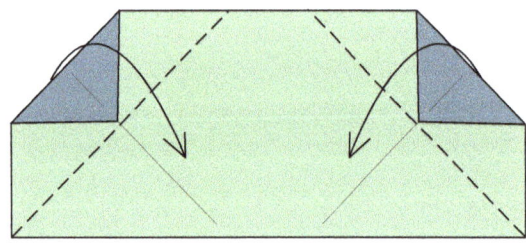

3. Valley fold along the existing creases.

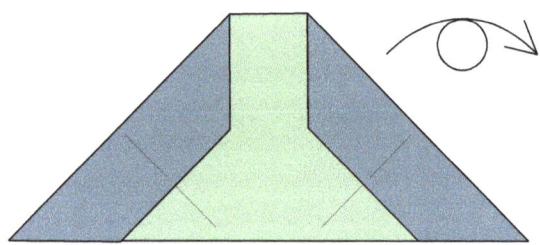

4. Turn over.

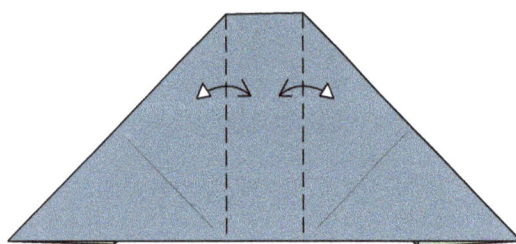

5. Precrease again.

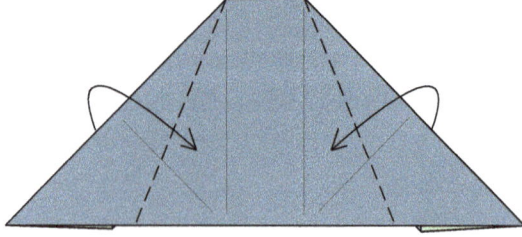

6. Valley fold the edges towards the creases, allowing the flaps from behind to swing towards the forefront.

mouney fold

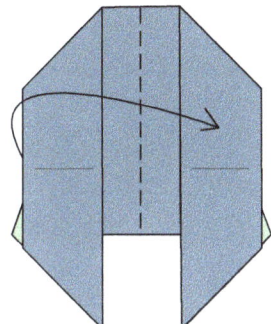

7. Valley fold in half.

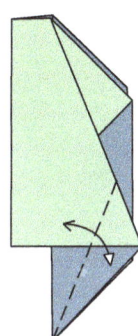

8. Precrease along the angle bisector.

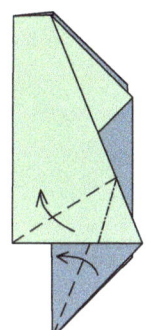

9. Swivel fold.

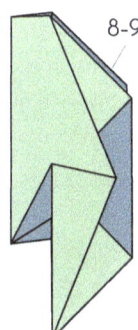

10. Repeat steps 8-9 behind.

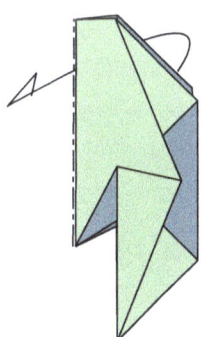

11. Swing the model open.

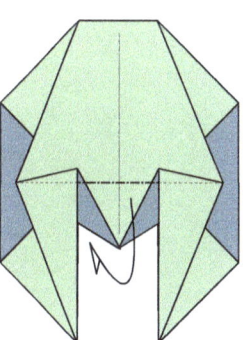

12. Mountain fold the flap.

mouney fold

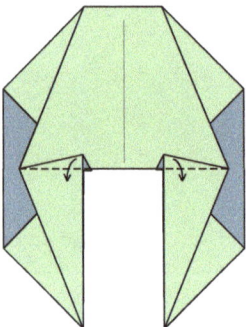

13. Valley fold the tiny flaps down.

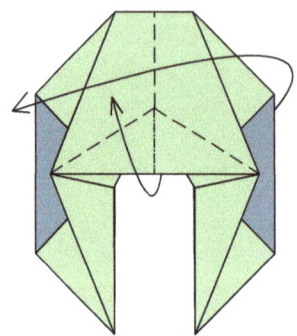

13. Valley fold over, while incorporating a reverse fold. The folds should follow the outline of the flap behind.

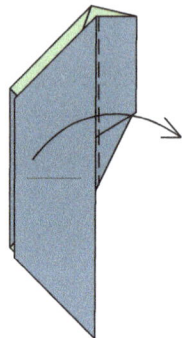

14. Valley fold one side over. A tiny squash fold should form naturally at the center.

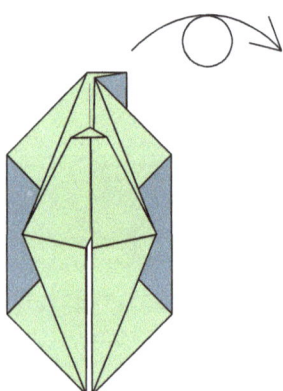

15. Turn over.

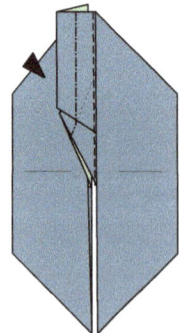

16. Squash the outer and inner flaps together.

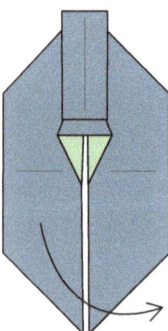

17. Bring one flap over the other. The model will become 3-D.

mouney fold

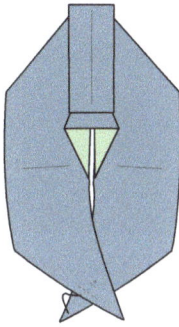 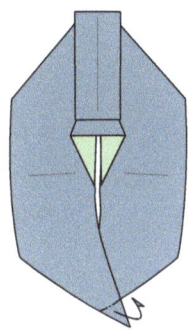 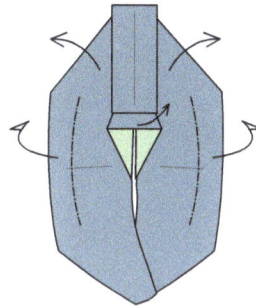

18. Valley fold the tip of the flap into the pocket behind.

19. Mountain fold the tip of the flap into the pocket behind.

20. Shape the model to taste.

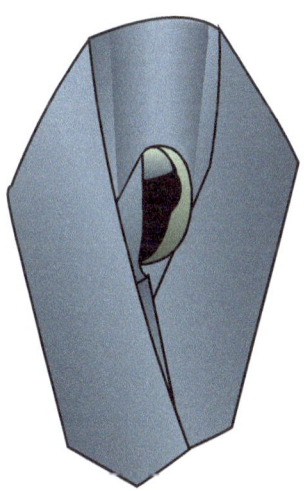

21. Completed *Mouney Fold*.

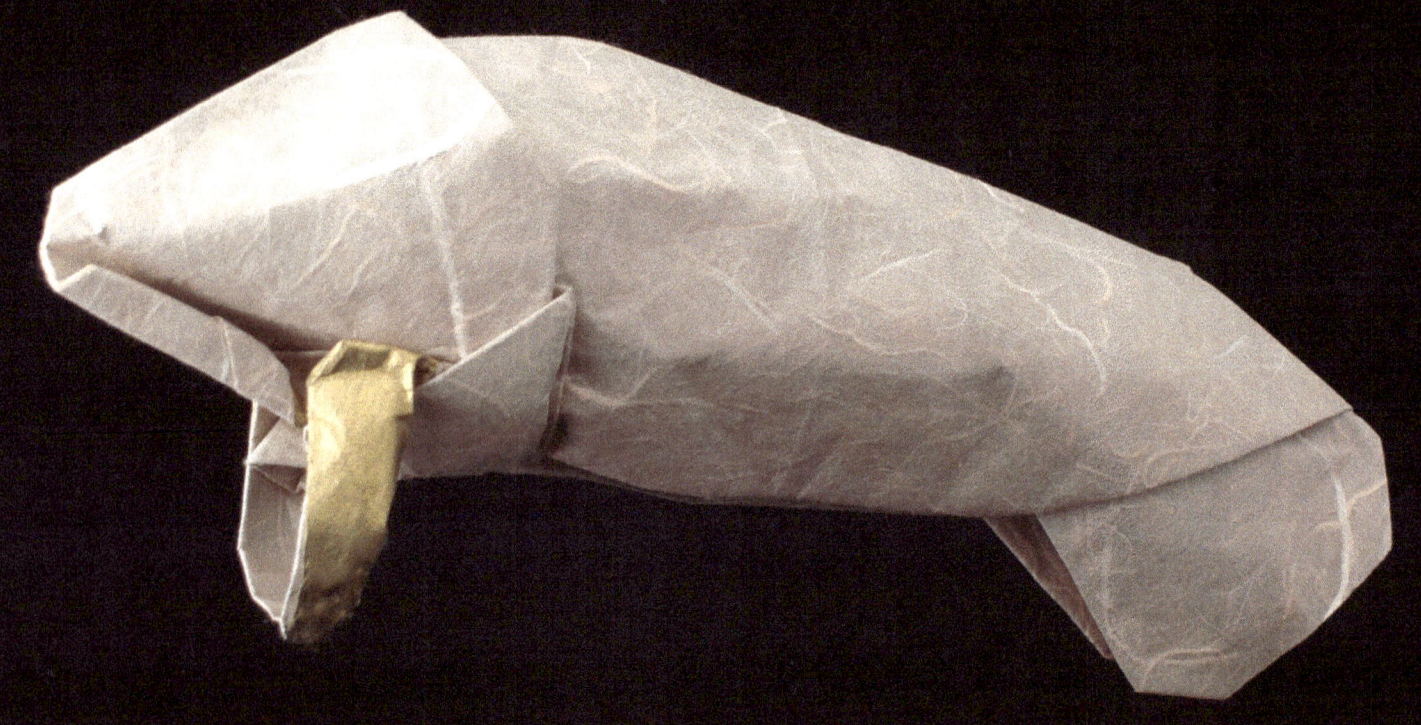

Prince Albert

About

As with most art forms, origami has its share of phallic representations. To stand out from the crowd, a little ornamentation is necessary. *Prince Albert* is based on the famous penile adornment. Ironically, the piercing was originally developed to secure the penis, and prevent unsightly bulges. However, once the willy is free, the flash of a gold hoop certainly draws attention. For this origami incarnation, the aspect ratio (girth to length relationship) creates a grand penile presence. This royal ratio can be attributed to orienting the chunky shaft along the side of the square (as opposed to a length-inducing diagonal orientation). Apropos to anything sporting a ring, a jewelry stand can be used to display this regal cock.

Tips

Once the model is completed, the lock from step thirty-two is secure, but it can come undone while performing the remainder of the steps. Exercise care while forming the ring, or you might have to replace the folds for the lock. For the final shaping, using a blunt object can help in opening the tip of the penis.

prince albert

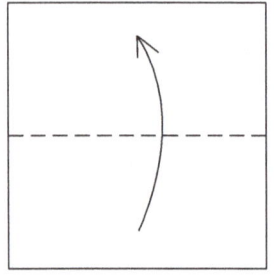

1. Valley fold in half (not too sharply).

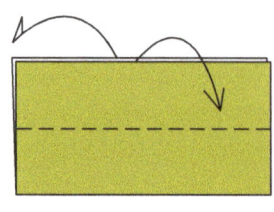

2. Valley fold the sides down.

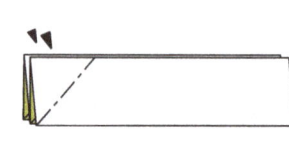

3. Reverse fold the two corners.

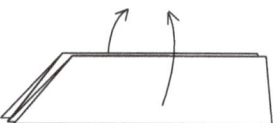

4. Unfold to step 2.

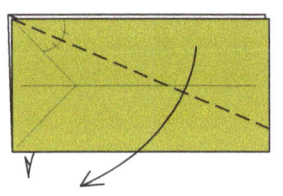

5. Valley fold the sides down.

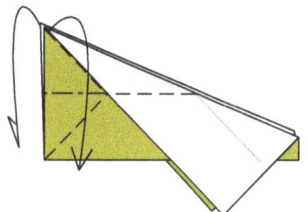

6. Swing down again while incorporating reverse folds.

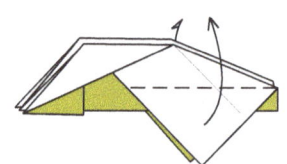

7. Valley fold the flaps up.

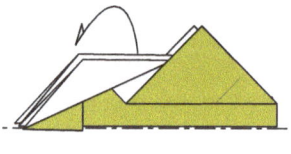

8. Open out the model symmetrically.

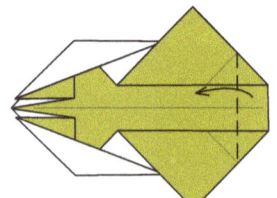

9. Valley fold in, using the precreases as a guide.

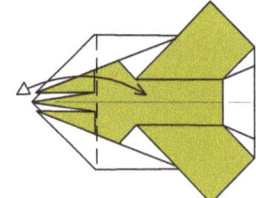

10. Precrease.

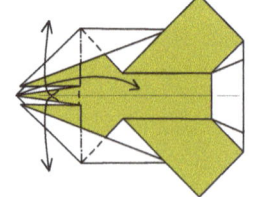

11. Swing over and squash flat.

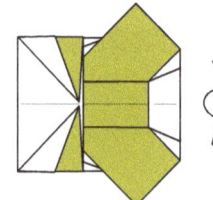

12. Turn over.

prince albert

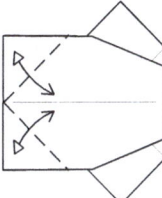

13. Precrease lightly.

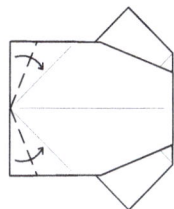

14. Valley fold over to the creases.

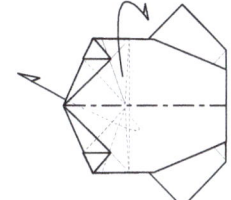

15. Mountain fold in half while pulling out the interior flaps. A tiny squash will naturally form along the interior walls.

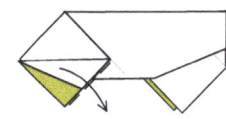

16. Unfold.

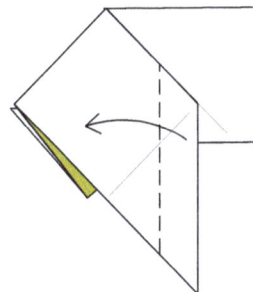

17. Valley fold over as far as possible.

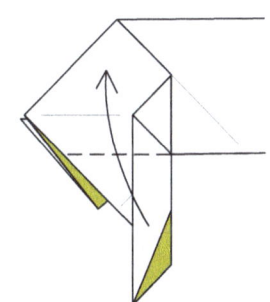

18. Valley fold up.

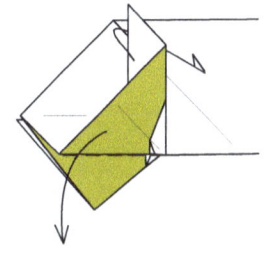

19. Unfold to step 17.

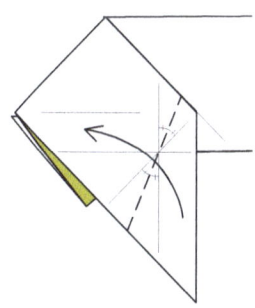

20. Valley fold through the angle bisectors.

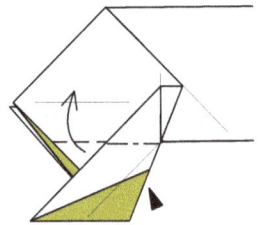

21. Reverse fold.

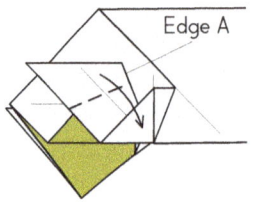

22. Valley fold, such that edge A lines up upon itself.

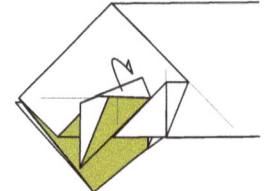

23. Wrap the single layer around.

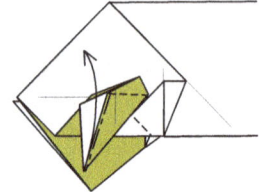

24. Squash fold upwards.

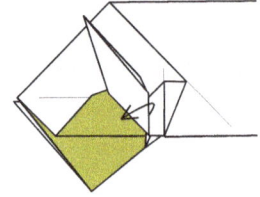

25. Pull out some paper and wrap around.

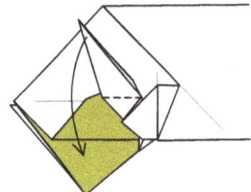

26. Swing back down.

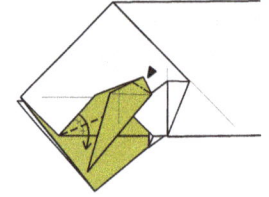

27. Swivel through.

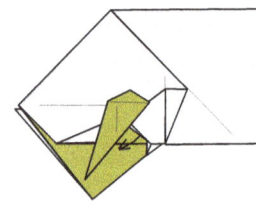

28. Slide out some paper.

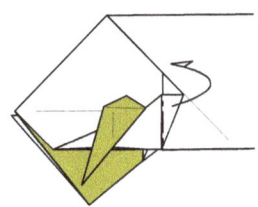

29. Mountain fold.

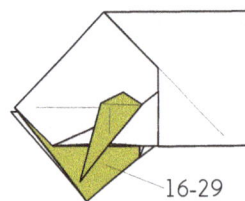

30. Repeat steps 16-29 behind.

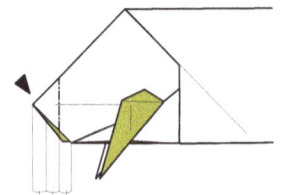

31. Reverse fold the tip approximately 2/3rds the way in.

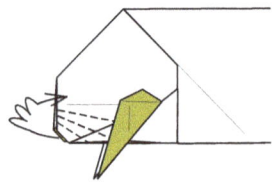

32. Roll the flap over and over to lock.

prince albert

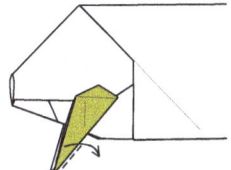

33. Open out the top layer. Do not repeat behind.

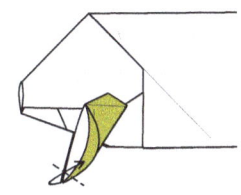

34. Valley fold the two flaps up together.

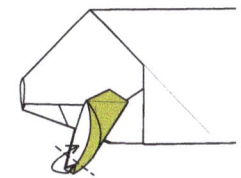

35. Valley fold up again.

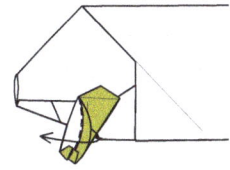

36. Close back up to lock.

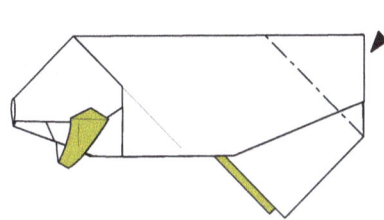

37. Reverse fold.

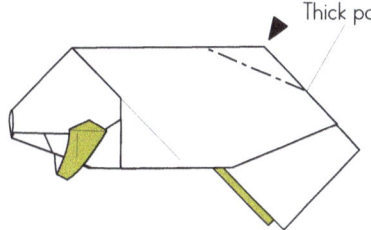

38. Closed sink, starting from the indicated thick point.

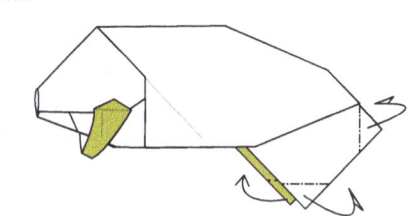

39. Mountain fold the corners in.

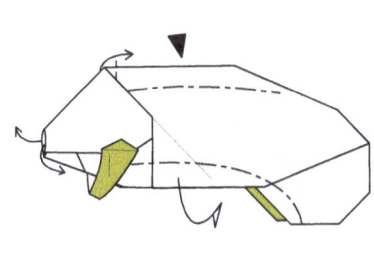

40. Shape the model to taste.

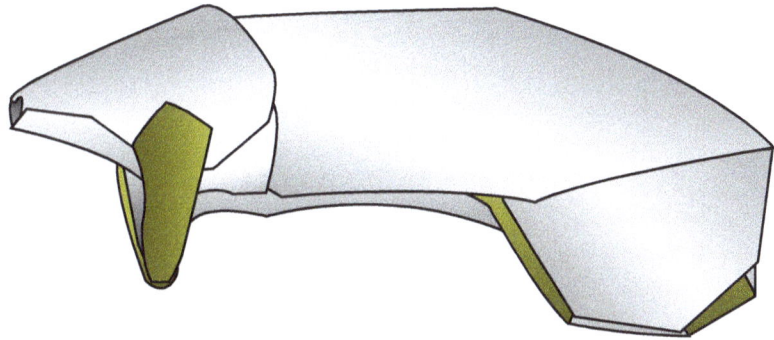

41. Completed *Prince Albert*.

47

Randy Rabbit

About

The very reproductive ability that has branded the rabbit as a garden pest has also made it a symbol of sexual behavior. Any aspiring Casanova has a benchmark to meet, whether he likes it or not. With its oversized haunches, the bunny seems engineered for mounting behavior. Considering this beast's reputation, even its erect, elongated ears seem phallic. For this origami incarnation, donning a bowtie gives this rabbit a sly disposition. You might not be surprised if the black neckband were all it is wearing. This bunny is based on the classic origami staring point, the Bird Base. Two of this base's appendages form the ears, and the remaining two form the bowtie and head. The cartoonish simplicity makes this piece iconic.

Tips

Steps thirty-two through thirty-four serve to form the rectangle that will become the bowtie. Some of these folds might be tricky to align perfectly, but you can always trim your rectangle with additional mountain folds in step thirty-four. Opening out the eye in step forty-four will require some artistic finesse. The lower portion of the eye is a bit deeper than the top area. Denting the lower edge will equalize the overall depth and help define the curve.

randy rabbit

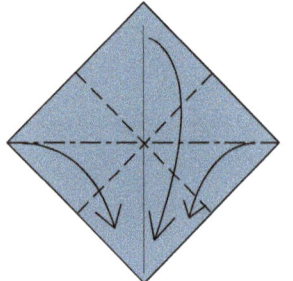

1. Collapse downwards.

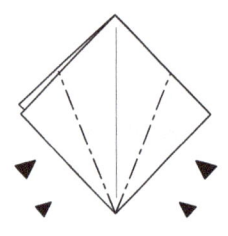

2. Reverse fold all four corners.

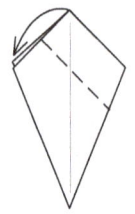

3. Lightly valley fold over.

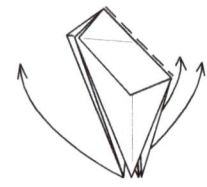

4. Open out the flaps. The flap at the left will be spread flat.

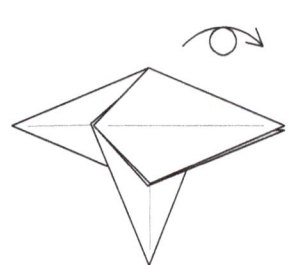

5. Turn over.

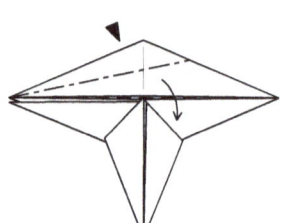

6. Spread squash along the angle bisector.

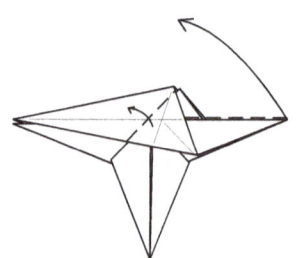

7. Open out the flap while swinging up.

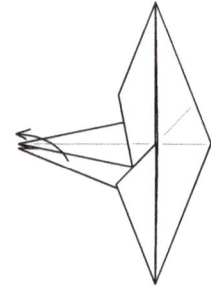

8. Pull the flap to the surface.

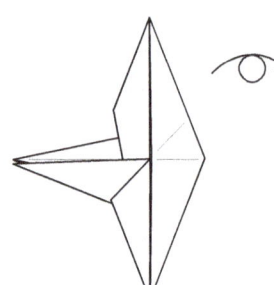

9. Turn over.

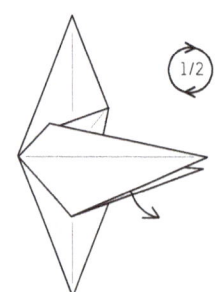

10. Undo the reverse fold. Rotate 1/2 turn.

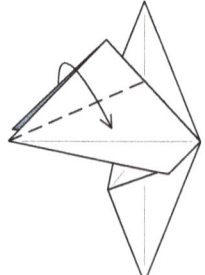

11. Valley fold down.

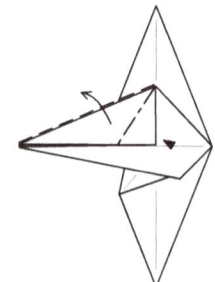

12. Squash fold.

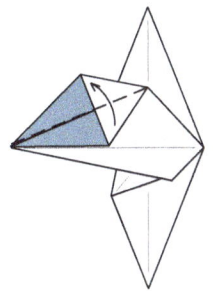
13. Valley fold up.

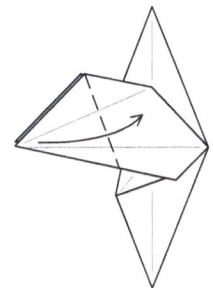
14. Lightly valley fold over.

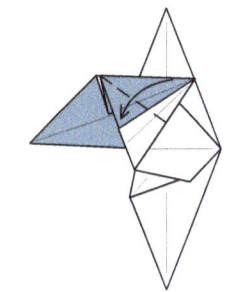
15. Valley fold over.

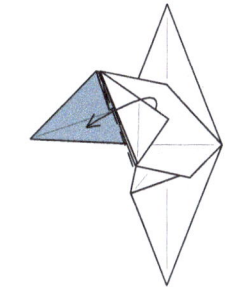
16. Swing over.

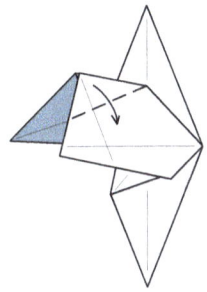
17. Valley fold down.

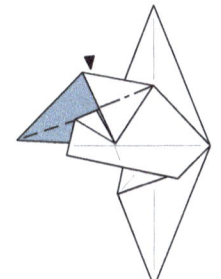
18. Reverse fold.

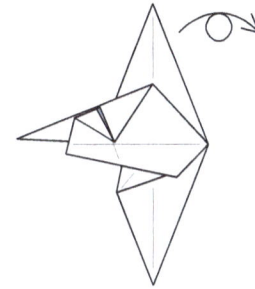
19. Turn over.

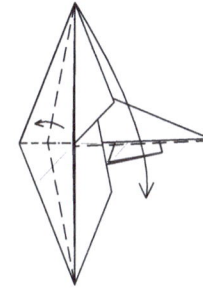
20. Swing down while incorporating a reverse fold.

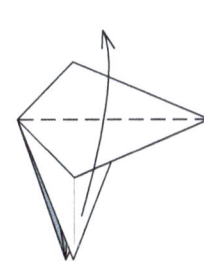
21. Swing back up. The model will not lie flat.

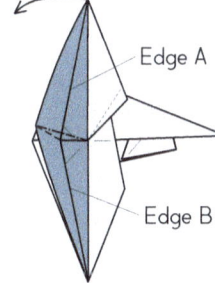
22. Slide over the flap, allowing edge A to align with edge B.

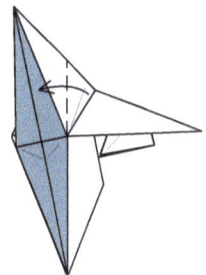
23. Valley fold over.

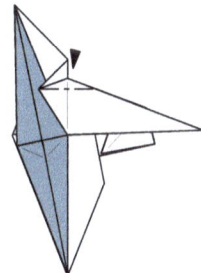
24. Sink the corner. You will have to open out the flap to accomplish this.

randy rabbit

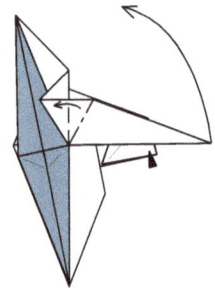

25. Squash fold.

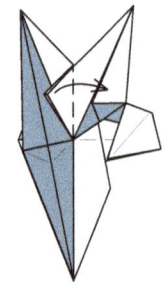

26. Valley fold over.

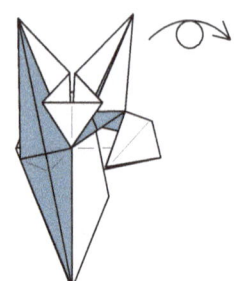

27. Turn over.

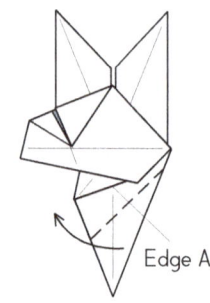

28. Valley fold over to edge A.

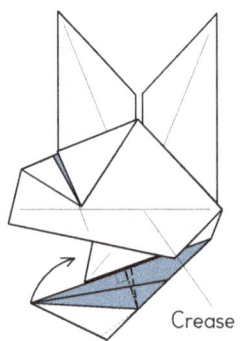

29. Swivel over so the top edge is parallel with Crease A.

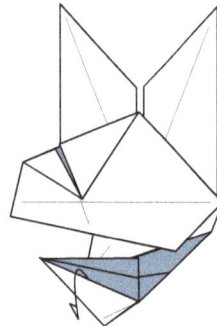

30. Wrap around the single layer.

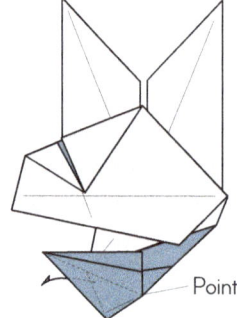

31. Slide out paper from behind, such that the resulting corner is even with point A.

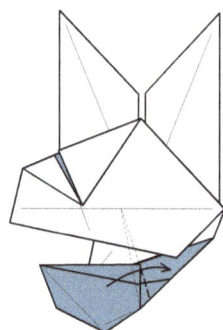

32. Form a tiny pleat on the colored layer only. The model will buckle slightly.

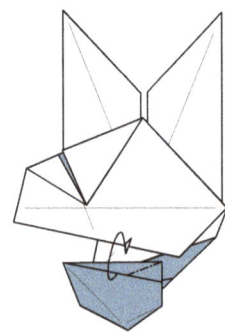

33. Wrap around a layer.

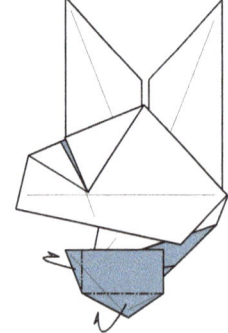

34. Shape with mountain folds.

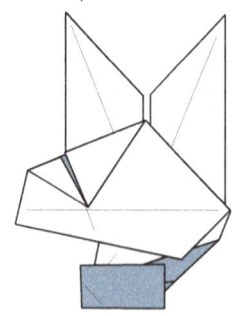

35. Turn over.

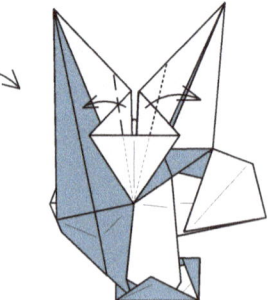

36. Valley in 1/3 at the left and 1/2 at the right.

randy rabbit

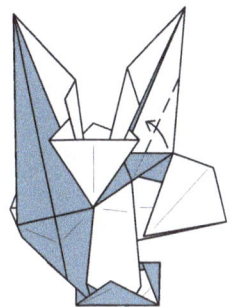

37. Valley fold over, tucking the flap underneath.

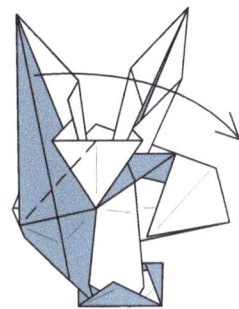

38. Valley fold as far as possible.

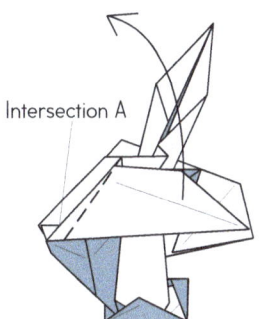

39. Valley fold, such that the upper edge hits intersection A.

40. Swivel over.

41. Valley fold over.

42. Turn over.

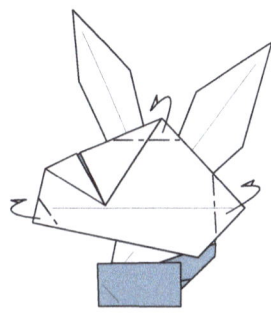

43. Shape with mountain folds.

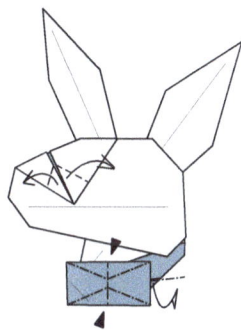

44. Shape the bowtie. Open out the eye.

45. Completed *Randy Rabbit*.

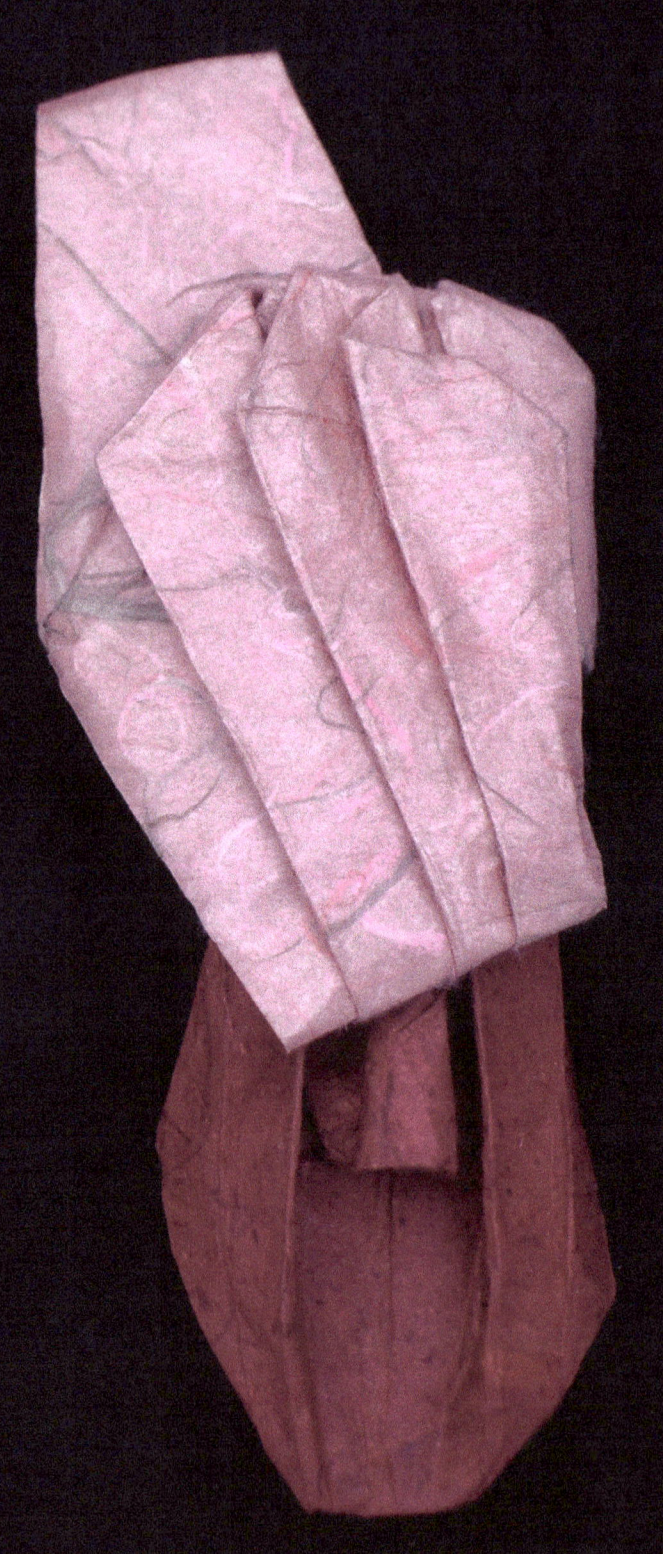

Taking a Hand in Female Matters

About

Elaborate pieces garner the most attention in art, but focusing on a subtle element can require the most skill. The human hand is one of the most difficult elements to express in any artistic medium, and origami is no exception. Adding female genitalia to the composition creates an ambiguous context; it is hard to tell if both components of the model belong to the same person. Initial renditions featured articulated fingers positioned closely together. To simplify the structure, the four main fingers were represented by a single flap. The folding sequence gives a pleated look, without expressly forming a pleat. Even more interesting is how the vagina is formed from opposite ends of the square. The clitoral area could have been formed from the labia region but making it an extension of the fingers ensures everything will be connected. Given the action depicted, maintaining a constant connection is a very good thing.

Tips

Step thirty-eight mentions there are no reference points for the pleat. Keep in mind however that the sides of this clitoral flap will have to slide into the labia section. If it is not a perfect fit, you can always fold the sides of the clitoral area behind. If you would like to make this in proportion with the male counterpart, using 13.3" paper is recommended.

— taking a hand in female matters —

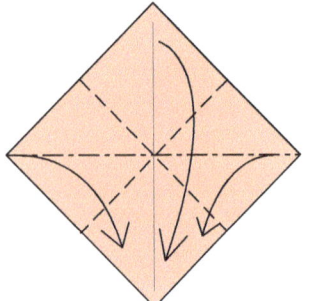

1. Collapse downwards.

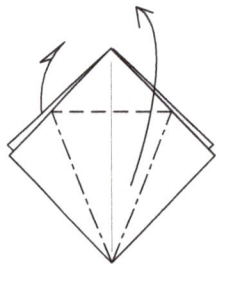

2. Petal fold up. Repeat behind.

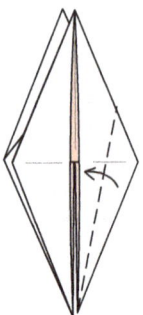

3. Valley fold over along the angle bisector.

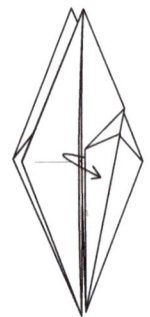

4. Wrap a single layer around to the surface (closed sinking the flap).

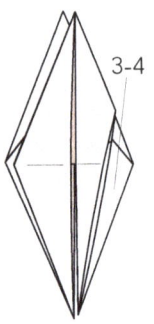

5. Repeat steps 3-4 behind.

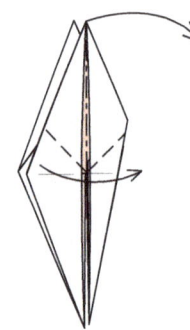

6. Swing over a layer while reverse folding the top flap.

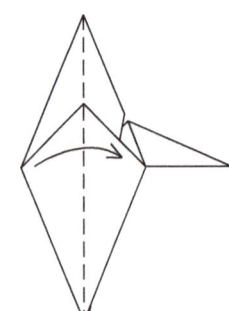

7. Valley fold over.

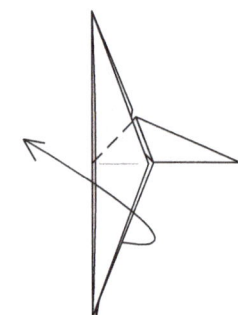

8. Valley fold to the left.

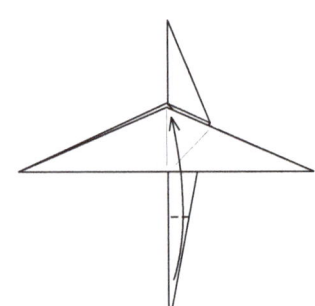

9. Valley fold up to meet the corner.

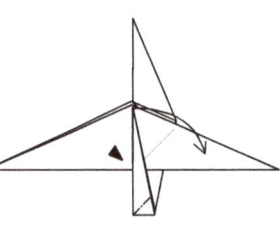

10. Squash fold, distributing the layers evenly.

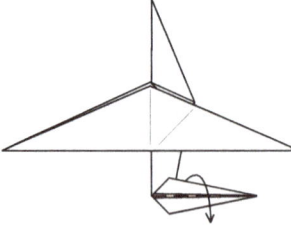

11. Valley fold in half.

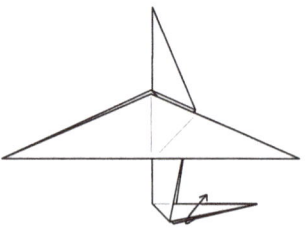

12. Wrap a single layer around to the surface.

taking a hand in female matters

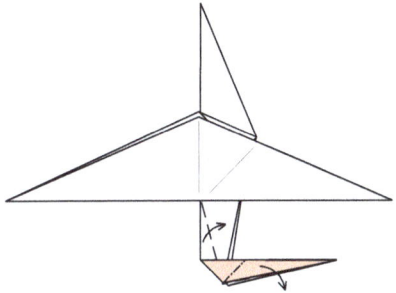

13. Swivel down a single layer.

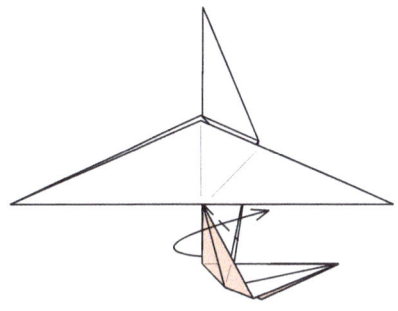

14. Repeat steps 12-13 behind.

15. Valley fold over to lie along the bottom of the triangular flap.

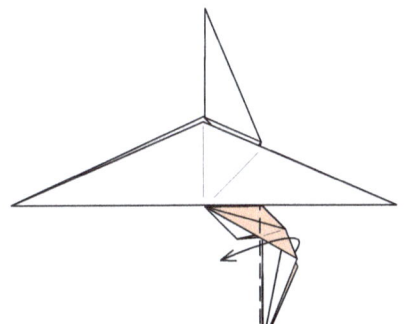

16. Spread apart the flap.

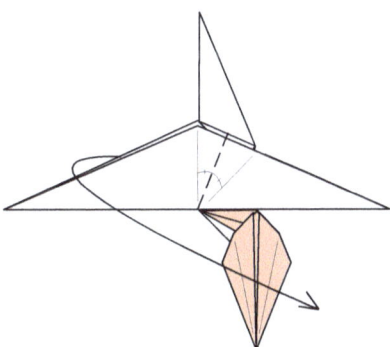

17. Valley fold down along the indicated angle bisector.

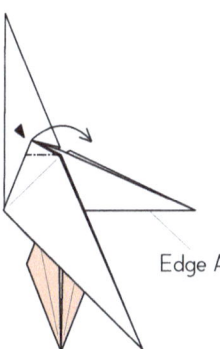

18. Reverse fold the two layers together, such that the resulting edge is parallel to edge A.

taking a hand in female matters

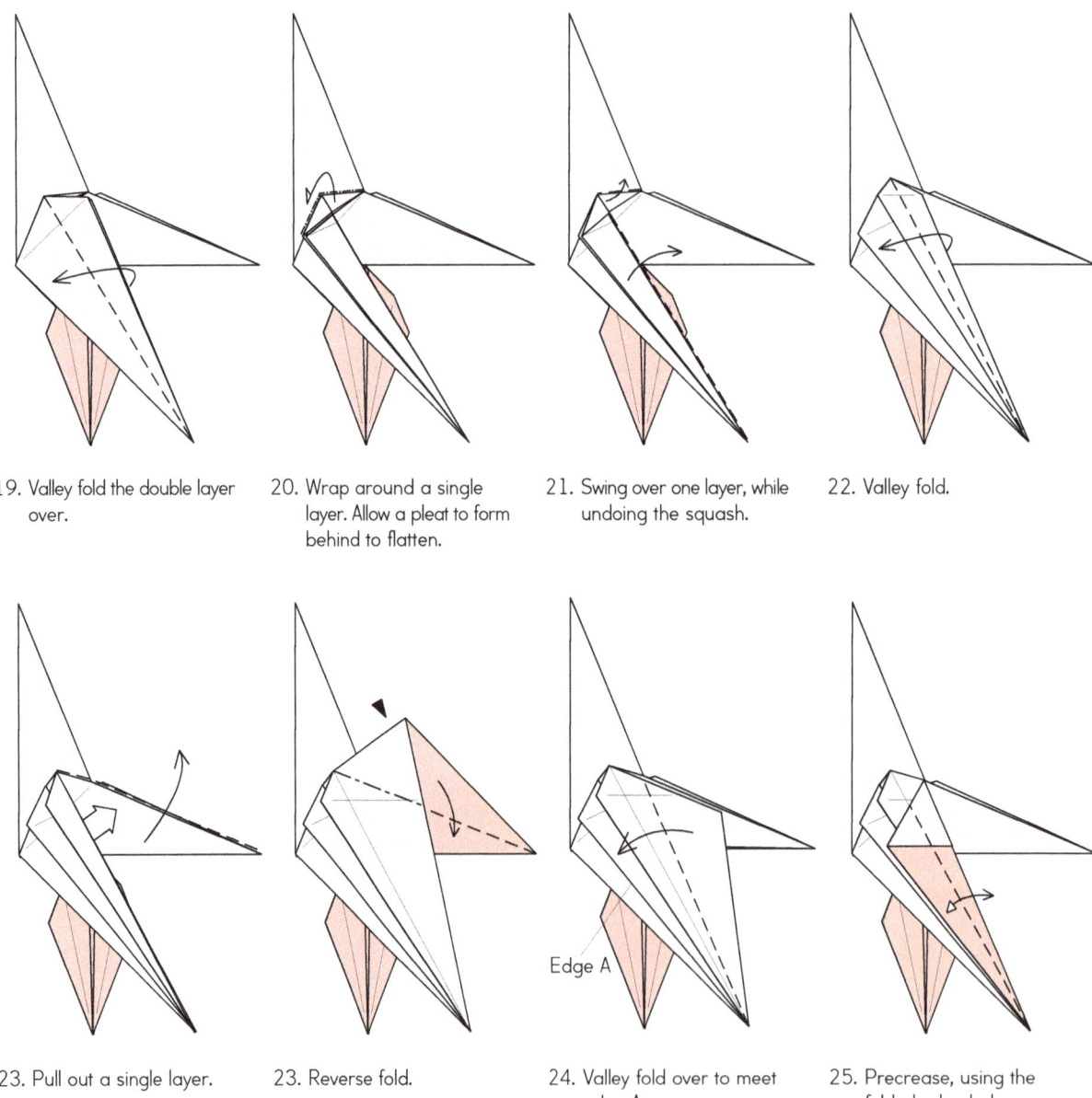

19. Valley fold the double layer over.

20. Wrap around a single layer. Allow a pleat to form behind to flatten.

21. Swing over one layer, while undoing the squash.

22. Valley fold.

23. Pull out a single layer.

23. Reverse fold.

24. Valley fold over to meet edge A.

25. Precrease, using the folded edge below as a guide.

———— taking a hand in female matters ————

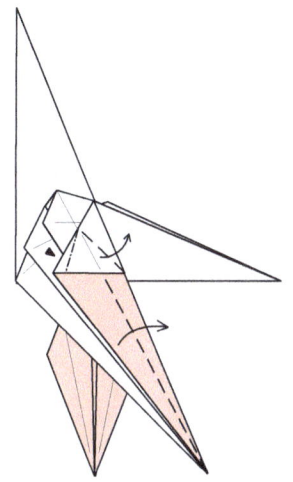

26. Squash fold as indicated.

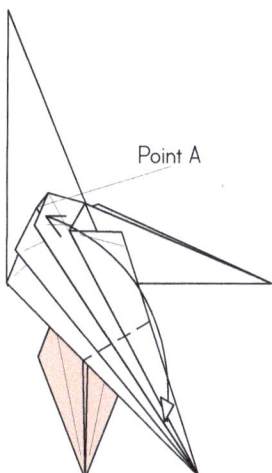

27. Precrease, such that the tip of the flap hits point A.

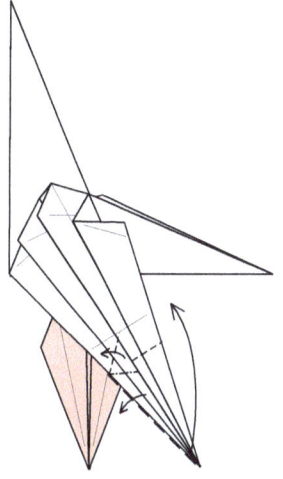

28. Swivel out along the angle bisector, allowing the flap to swing upwards. Note that the fold begins beneath the center pleat.

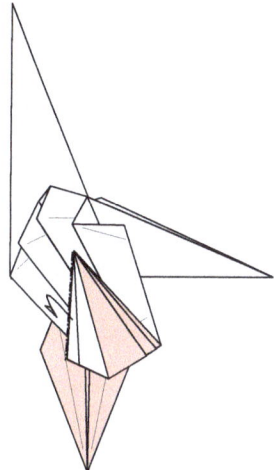

29. Wrap a single layer around.

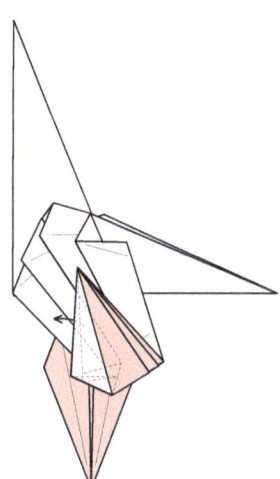

30. Pull out the hidden edge as far as possible, allowing a swivel to form.

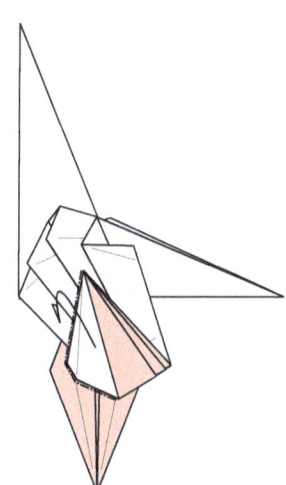

31. Wrap the single layer around.

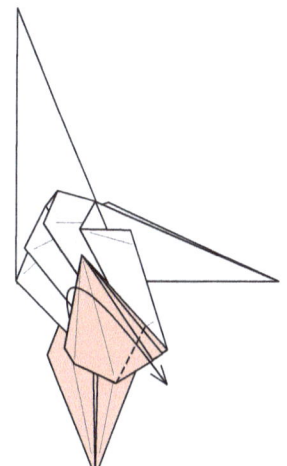

32. Lightly swing the flap down.

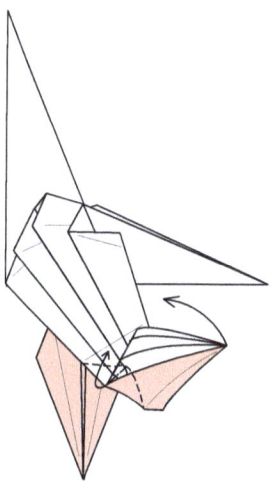

33. Close back up, while reverse folding the single layer up.

taking a hand in female matters

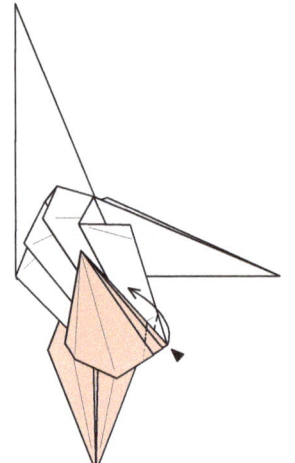

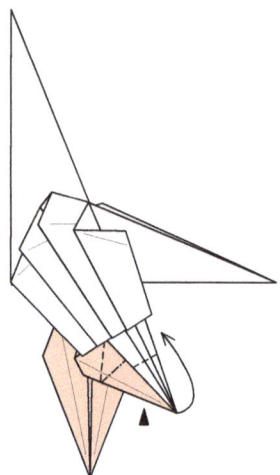

34. Reverse fold.

35. Sink the corner, to meet the edge of the flap folded in step 33.

36. Form a mountain fold slightly above the colored region.

37. Squash fold, so that the raw edge falls underneath the fingers.

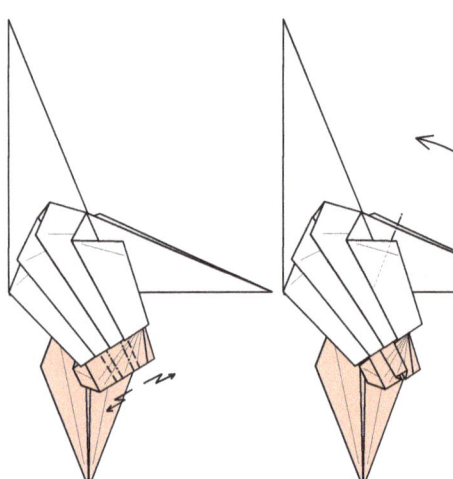
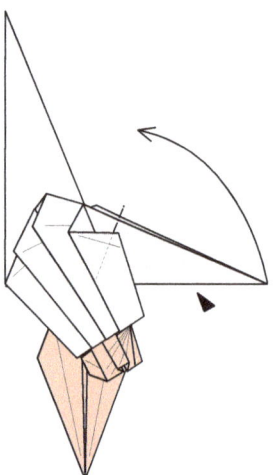
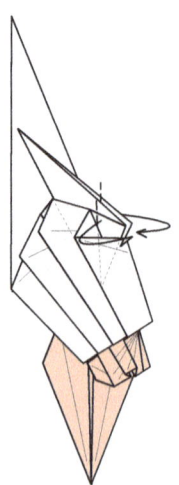
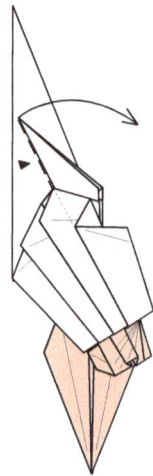

38. Pleat the colored section. There are no reference points for this.

39. Reverse fold along the angle bisector.

40. Fold the sides in along the angle bisector.

41. Reverse fold the point outwards.

taking a hand in female matters

42. Outside reverse fold.

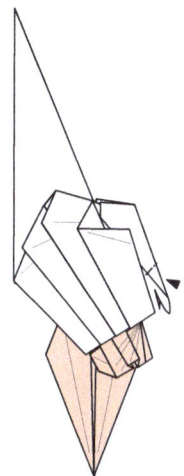

43. Reverse fold the tip.

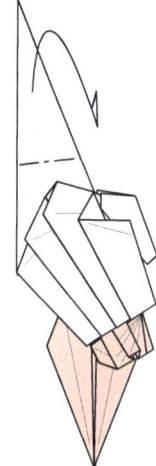

44. Mountain fold to taste.

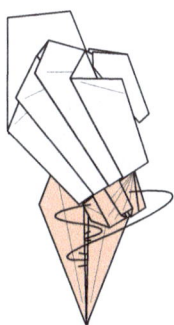

45. Tuck the flaps into the pockets. The hand will rotate slightly.

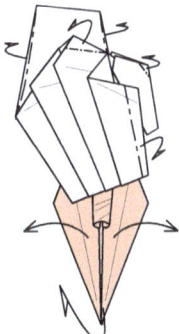

46. Pull at the sides of the vagina, and shape to taste. Shape the hand to taste with mountain folds.

47. Completed *Taking a Hand in Female Matters*.

Taking a Hand in Male Matters

About

Developed concurrently with its female counterpart, *Taking a Hand in Male Matters* continues the theme of helping hands. Representing different genitalia and using a different hand position makes for a very different model. Still, creating the hand was the most difficult element. Positioning an opposable thumb is tricky, and any miss-alignment of the hand parts will cause the model to look awkward. Using thirds for the hand crept into the penis portion, resulting in an asymmetrical folding sequence for the testicles. After fifty or so steps of folding, you can have a model that might raise a few heads (in the course of raising its own).

Tips

Keep in mind the fold in step twenty-nine is a temporary position for the cluster of fingers; so, do not fold too sharply. Positioning the hand elements is an artistic challenge. To make the pose seem natural, it is important to position the four main fingers below the thumb. If you would like to make this in proportion with the female counterpart, using 16" paper is recommended.

— taking a hand in male matters —

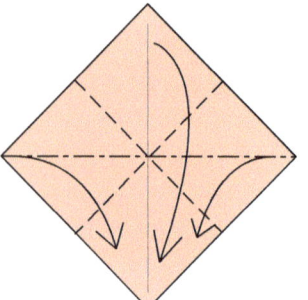

1. Collapse downwards.

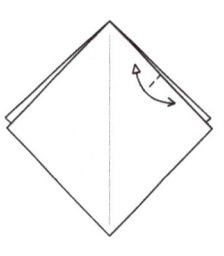

2. Pinch halfway.

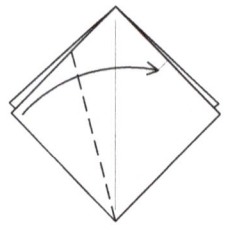

3. Valley fold over, such that the corner hits the crease.

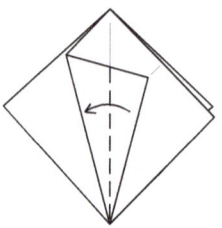

4. Valley fold over to the folded edge.

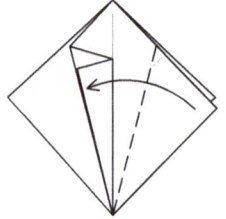

5. Valley fold over to the cluster of edges.

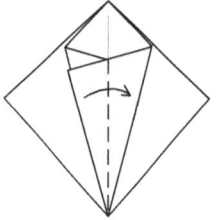

6. Valley fold over to the folded edge.

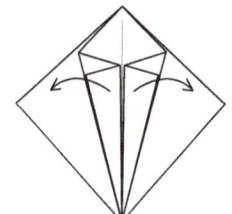

7. Unfold the pleats.

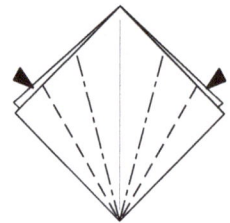

8. Reverse fold in and then out along the existing creases.

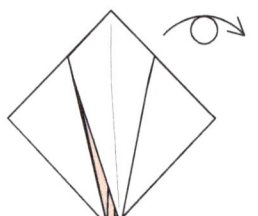

9. Turn over.

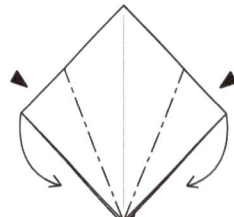

10. Reverse fold the sides.

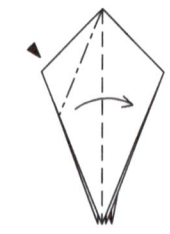

11. Valley fold over and spread squash.

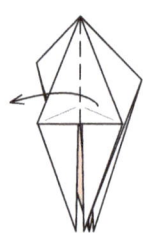

12. Valley fold over one flap.

— taking a hand in male matters —

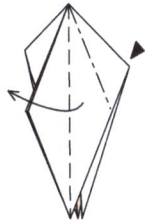

13. Spread squash again.

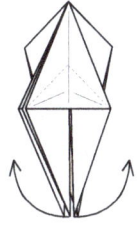

14. Reverse fold the top flaps outwards.

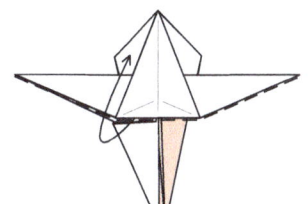

15. Wrap around a single layer.

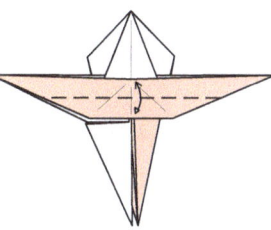

16. Precrease the flap in half.

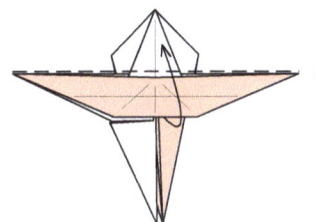

17. Swing the flap up.

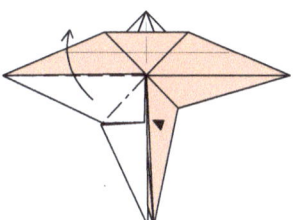

18. Valley fold up and squash.

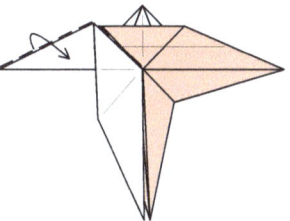

19. Wrap around a single layer.

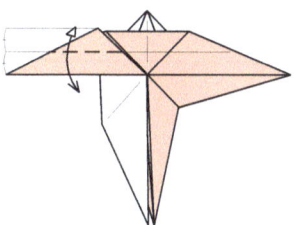

20. Precrease the top flap in half.

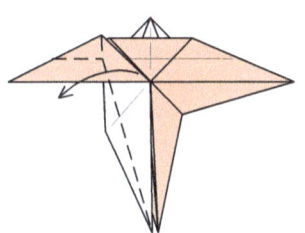

21. Valley fold over as far as possible (note that the fold changes its angle at the top). Model will not lie flat.

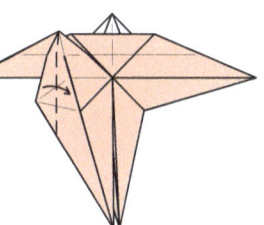

22. Valley fold along the angle bisector.

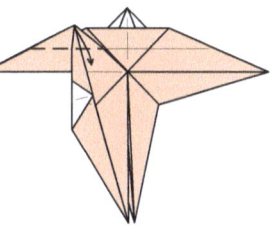

23. Valley fold down, allowing the model to flatten.

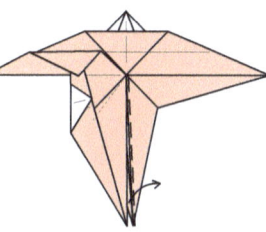

24. Swivel a single layer over.

— taking a hand in male matters —

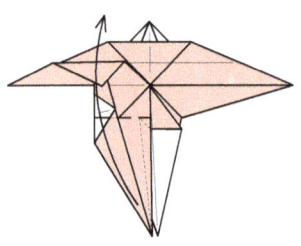

25. Valley fold up, so as to allow the hidden single layer to squash flat.

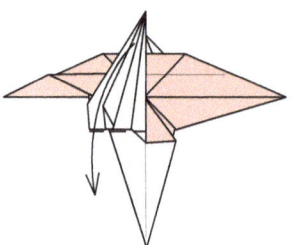

26. Swing back down.

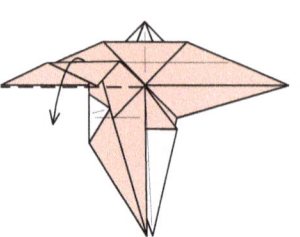

27. Valley fold one flap down.

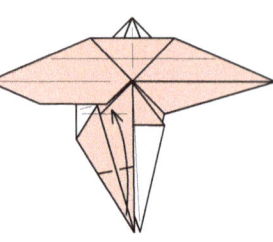

28. Valley fold the point to the corner.

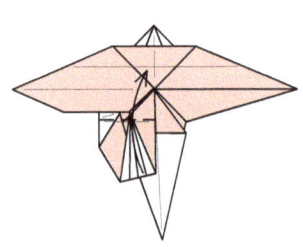

29. Valley fold up, so the corner hits the crease.

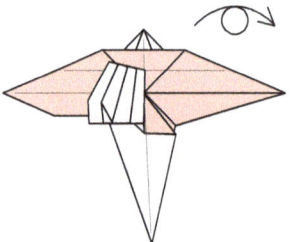

30. Turn over.

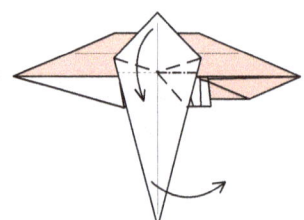

31. Valley fold down the top, while swiveling over the bottom (form the top valley folds first).

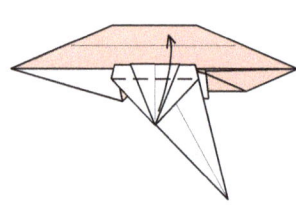

32. Valley fold up.

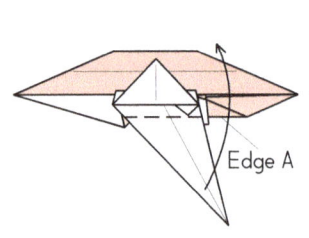

33. Valley fold up, so as to be in alignment with edge A.

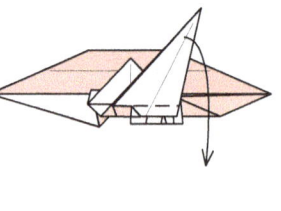

34. Valley fold down.

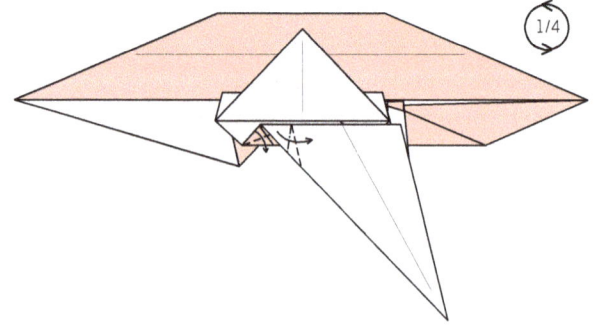

35. Swivel over. Rotate the model.

taking a hand in male matters

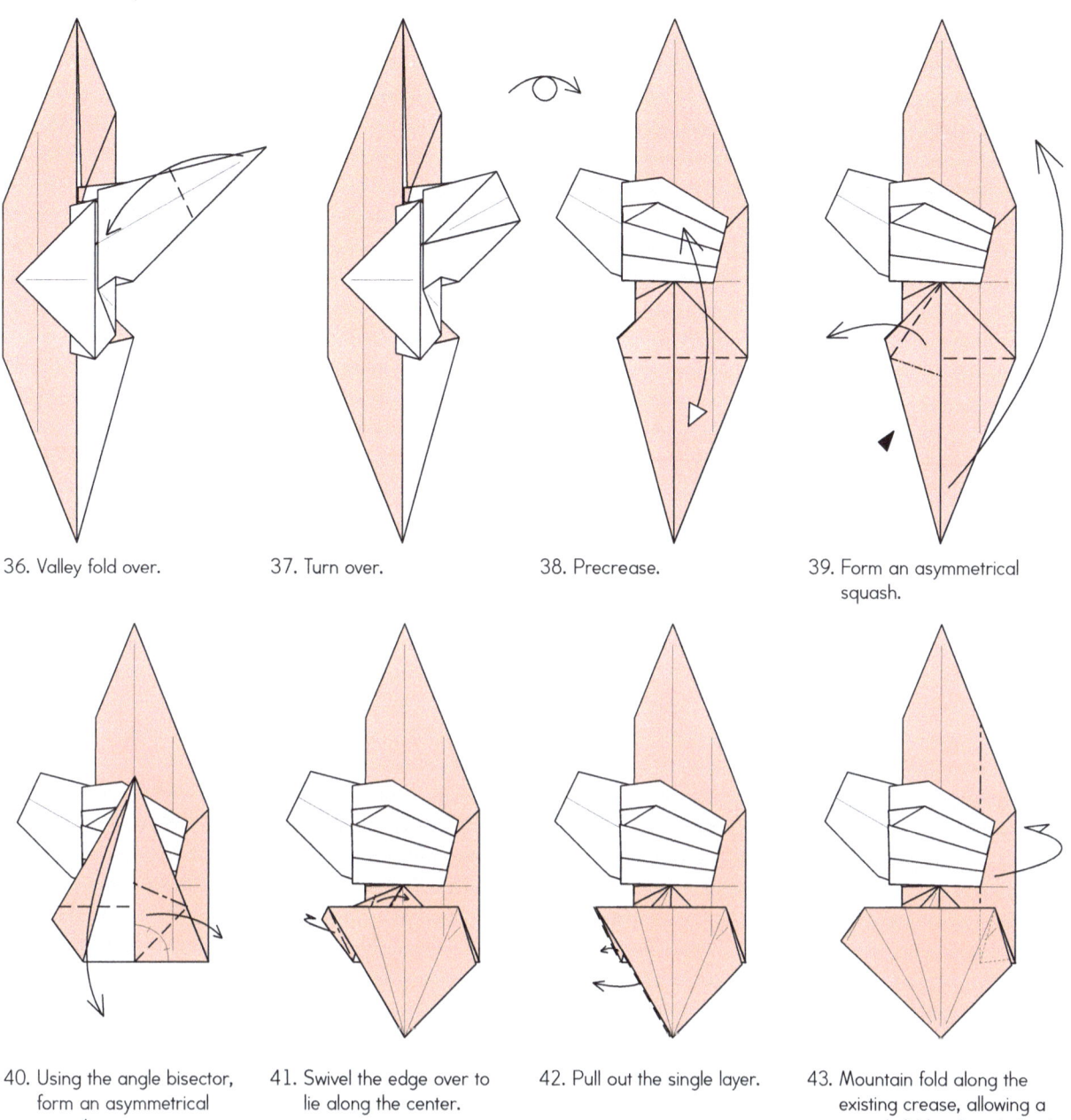

36. Valley fold over.

37. Turn over.

38. Precrease.

39. Form an asymmetrical squash.

40. Using the angle bisector, form an asymmetrical squash.

41. Swivel the edge over to lie along the center.

42. Pull out the single layer.

43. Mountain fold along the existing crease, allowing a squash fold to form behind.

taking a hand in male matters

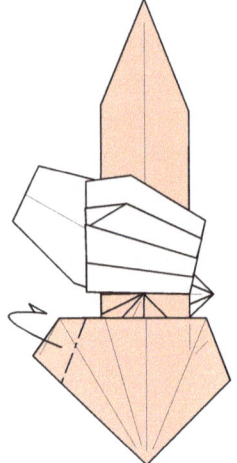

44. Mountain fold the left edge, so that it mirrors the corresponding right edge.

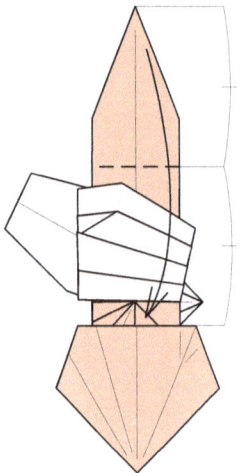

45. Valley fold down.

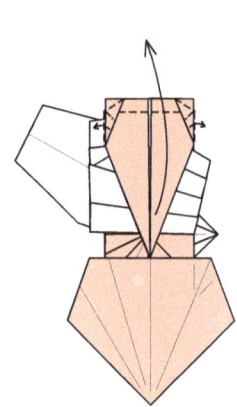

46. Valley fold up, while swiveling out the sides.

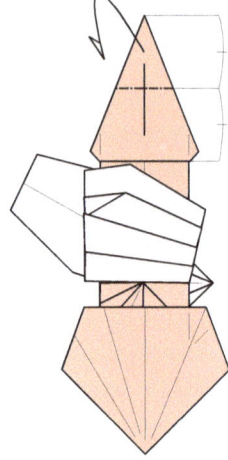

47. Mountain fold the top.

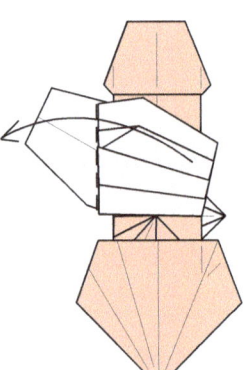

48. Swing the flap over.

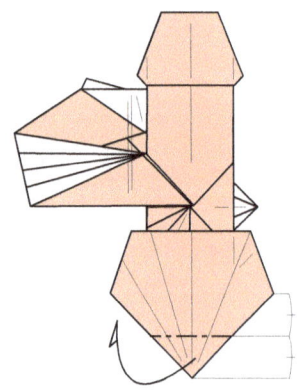

49. Mountain fold the bottom.

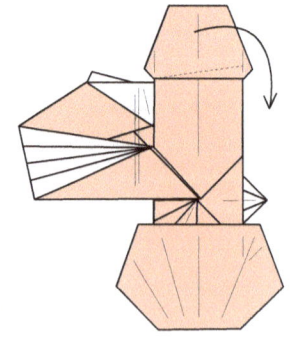

50. Alter the hidden pleat, so the top tilts slightly.

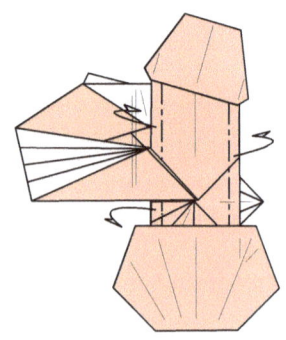

51. Round the sides with mountain folds.

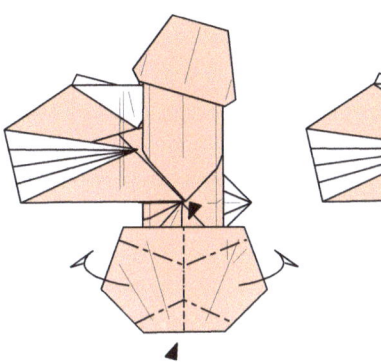
52. Shape the bottom with mountain folds, and make it three-dimensional.

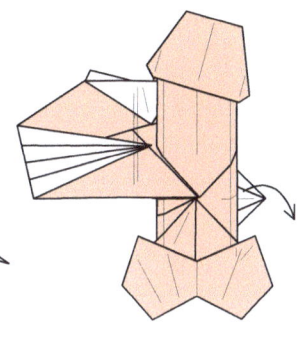
53. Pull out the side corner. Some of the back will come undone, and not lie completely flat.

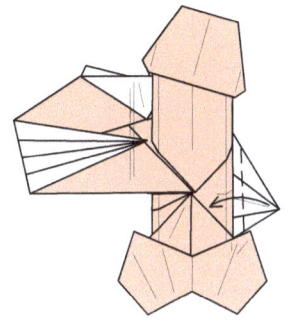
54. Valley fold over.

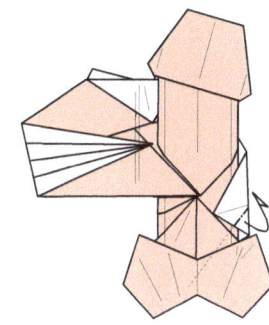
55. Mountain fold.

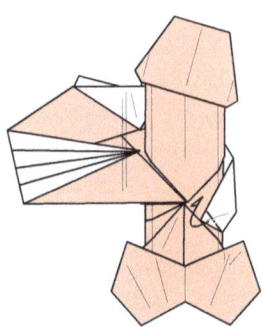
56. Mountain fold again.

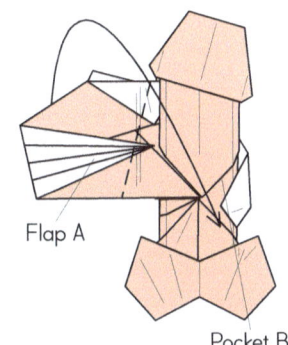
57. Valley fold over. Optionally, you can twist flap A into pocket B.

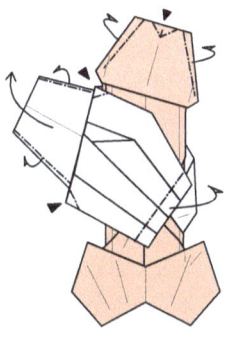
58. Shape the model with reverse folds and mountain folds as indicated.

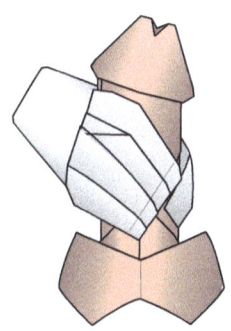
59. Completed *Taking a Hand in Male Matters*.

The Missionary

About

Mistaken identity can be a good thing. When *The Missionary* debuted in 1996, designing origami bugs was the craze. Having more than just one set of legs and arms caused several people to presume the piece to be an insect. Closer inspection revealed the appendages to be human in origin, but that did not prevent this couple to be taken as co-ed wrestlers. As one of the earliest examples of sexually-oriented origami, staying low on the origami radar kept this model out of trouble. The low profile was short-lived, as *The Missionary* was soon to be featured in a television show and in a half-dozen magazines. Most of the folds used are straightforward, which increased the model's popularity in the origami community with its accessibility. The structure is subtly interesting, as it starts off symmetrically, but you soon realize the two sets of legs are formed very differently. The woman's legs are from the corners of the square, while the man's legs originate from the middle portion of the paper. See if you can determine when the model becomes asymmetrical.

Tips

In step twenty-one, the closed-sink will tend to pull the top flap down. If this happens, simply valley fold the flap back up. Structurally, the woman's hair is not symmetrical; so, do not be surprised when folding that section. The most important finishing touch is positioning the two heads, so they are gazing at each other. You might have to adjust the crimps in the necks to accomplish this.

the missionary

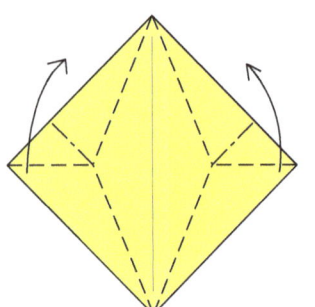

1. Form rabbit ears on both sides.

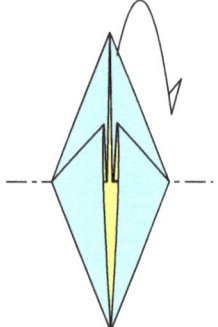

2. Swing the flap back.

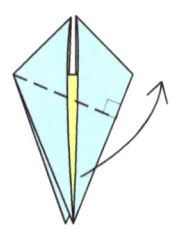

3. Valley fold up.

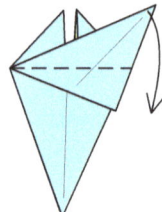

4. Valley fold down.

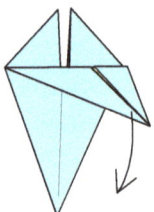

5. Unfold.

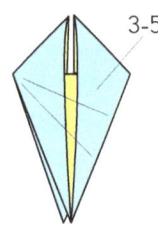

6. Repeat steps 3-5 in mirror image.

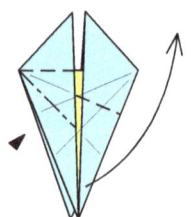

7. Form an asymmetrical squash.

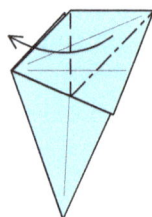

8. Squash fold again.

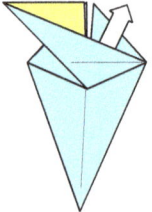

9. Pull out a single layer to make the sides symmetrical.

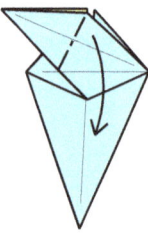

10. Squash fold.

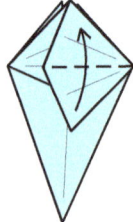

11. Valley fold up.

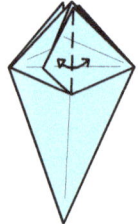

12. Precrease.

the missionary

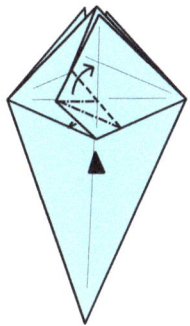 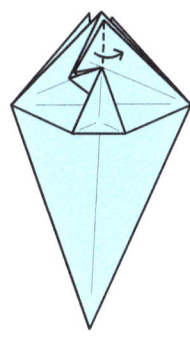 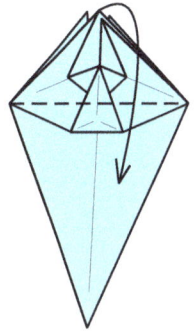 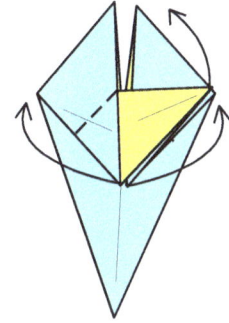

13. Valley fold the flap to hit the center, allowing a squash to form at the bottom.

14. Pull one layer through.

15. Swing the top section down.

16. Spread apart the flap.

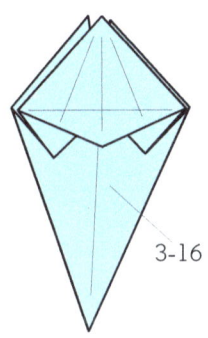 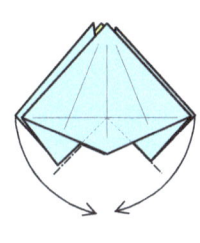 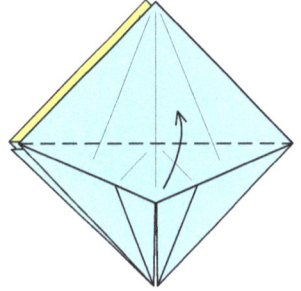 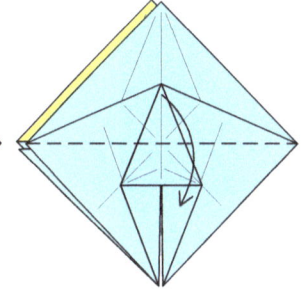

17. Repeat steps 3-16 behind.

18. Reverse fold the center flaps down (this will bring down the top center flaps as well).

19. Valley fold up, releasing the trapped layers.

20. Valley fold back down.

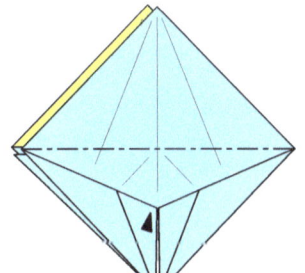 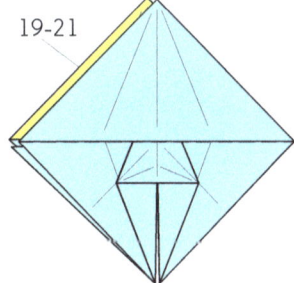 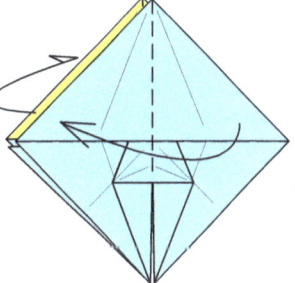 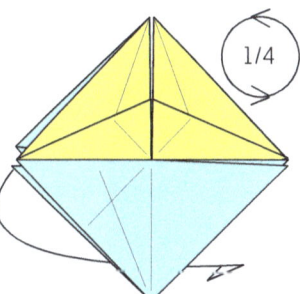

21. Closed sink upwards.

22. Repeat steps 19-21 behind.

23. Swing the large flaps over as indicated.

24. Swing the back flap over. Rotate the model.

73

the missionary

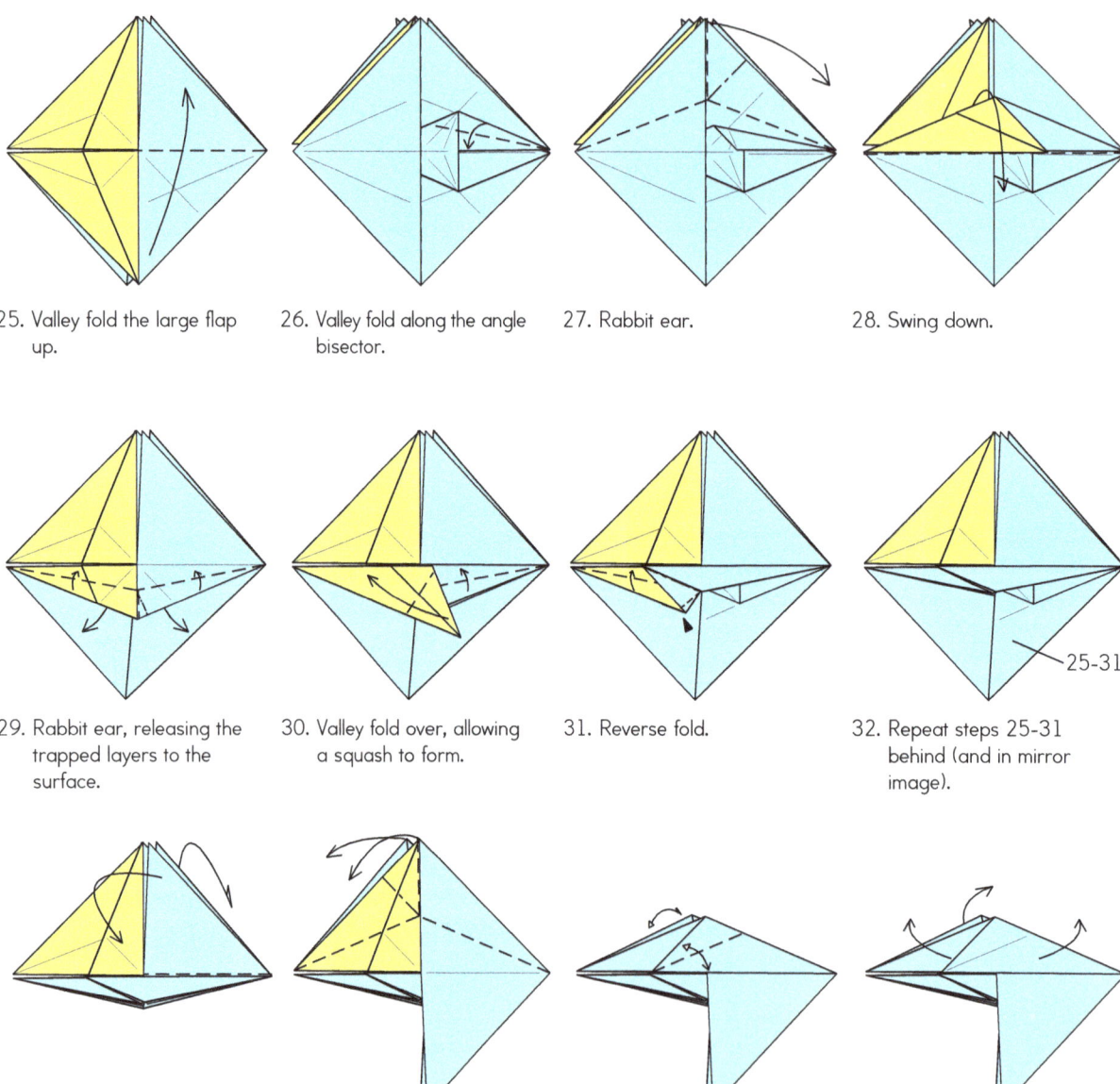

25. Valley fold the large flap up.

26. Valley fold along the angle bisector.

27. Rabbit ear.

28. Swing down.

29. Rabbit ear, releasing the trapped layers to the surface.

30. Valley fold over, allowing a squash to form.

31. Reverse fold.

32. Repeat steps 25-31 behind (and in mirror image).

33. Swing the flaps down.

34. Rabbit ear the top flaps.

35. Precrease along the angle bisector. Repeat behind.

36. Unfold the top rabbit ears.

the missionary

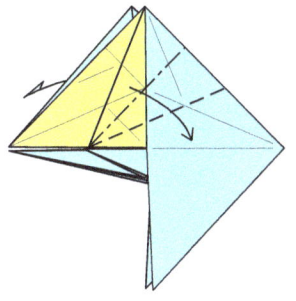

37. Crimp the sides down.

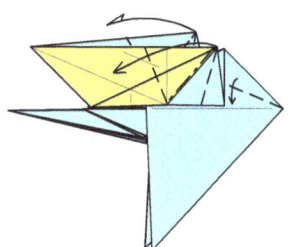

38. Stretch the point over. Repeat behind.

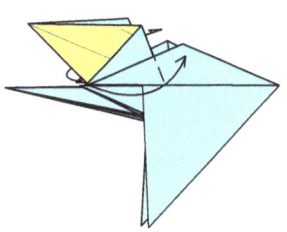

39. Swing the flaps back up.

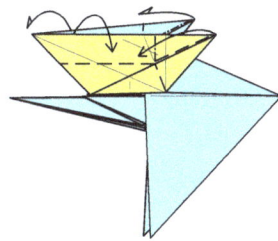

40. Outside reverse fold, while swinging the flaps back over.

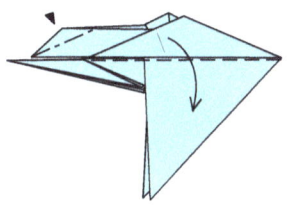

41. Spread apart the sides, allowing a spread squash to form.

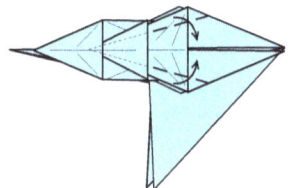

42. Valley fold the top layers in. These folds should be approximately along angle trisectors.

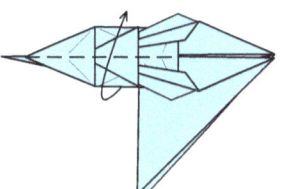

43. Close back up.

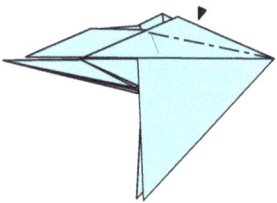

44. Sink along the angle bisector.

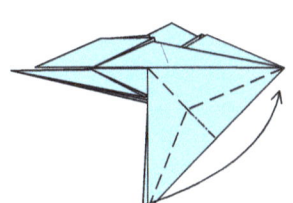

45. Rabbit ear the large flap.

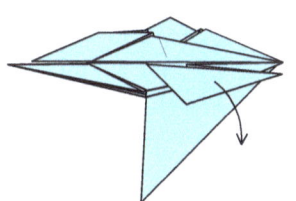

46. Unfold the rabbit ear.

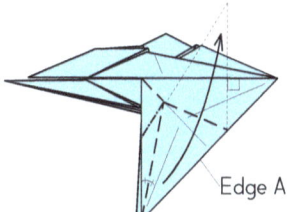

47. Form an offset rabbit ear, letting edge A lie at a right angle.

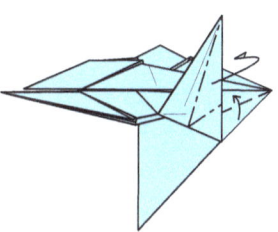

48. Swivel in.

75

— the missionary —

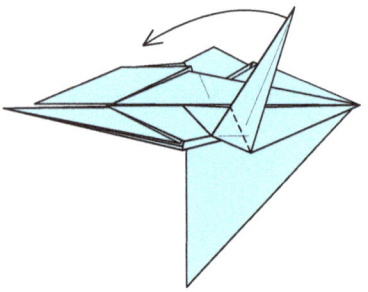

49. Lightly swing over.

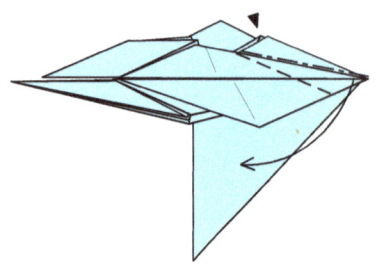

50. Pleat down, allowing paper to slide out at the top. See the next step for approximate positioning.

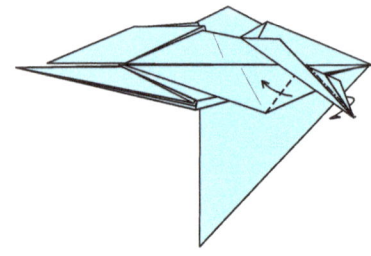

51. Swivel in.

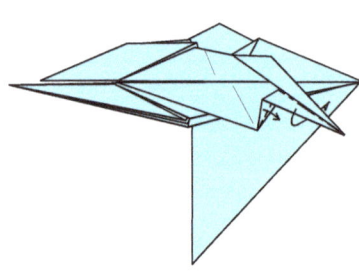

52. Swivel again, this time into the interior of the flap.

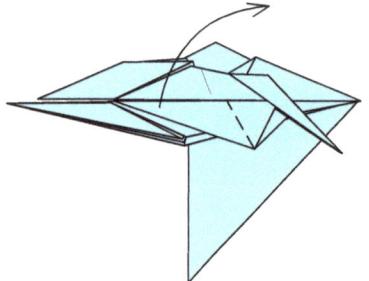

53. Swing back up.

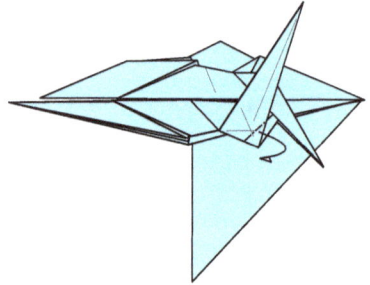

54. Mountain fold to taste.

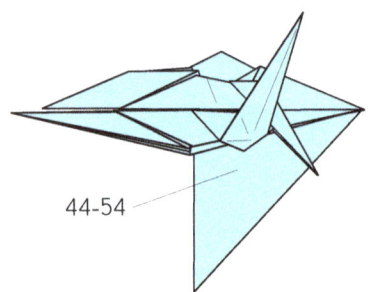

44-54

55. Repeat steps 44-54 behind (and in mirror image).

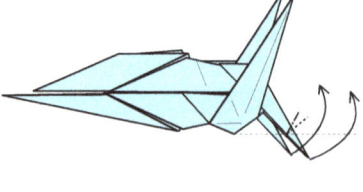

56. Crimp upwards, to lie on the same plane as the rest of the model.

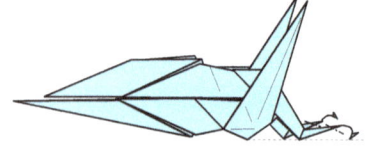

57. Squash fold the points down.

the missionary

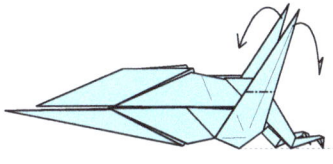

58. Mountain fold the two points down.

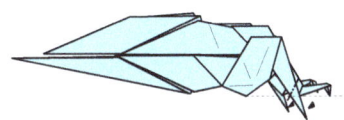

59. Squash fold the tips.

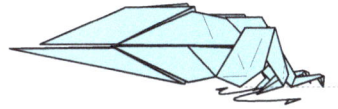

60. Stretch the tips back, ensuring alignment with the rest of the model.

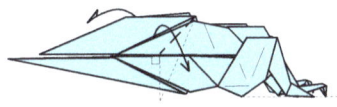

61. Valley fold the points down, such that the left edges lie at a right angle.

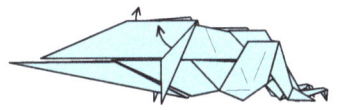

62. Pull out a single layer from each flap.

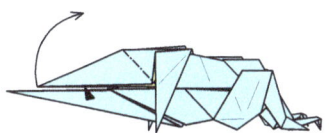

63. Reverse fold upwards.

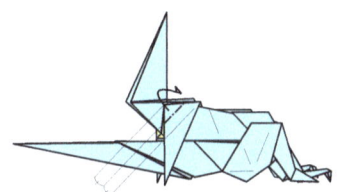

64. Mountain fold the corner. Repeat behind.

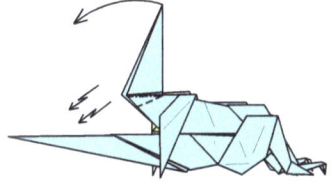

65. Crimp the top flap down.

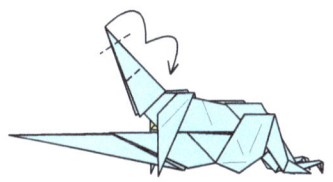

66. Outside reverse fold the tip to meet the base of the triangle.

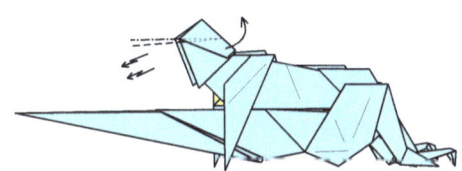

67. Form a tiny crimp.

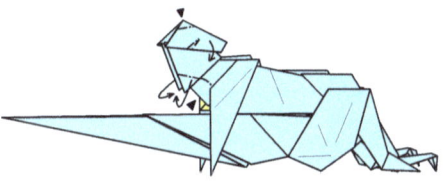

68. Shape the hair with a reverse fold and crimp. Mountain fold the chin, and shape the neck.

the missionary

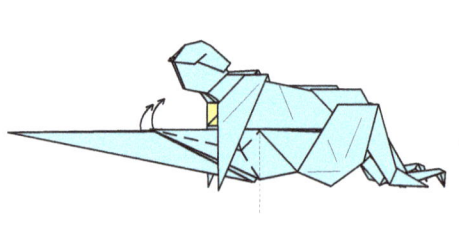

69. Rabbit ear the arms to lie along the imaginary line.

70. Outside reverse fold.

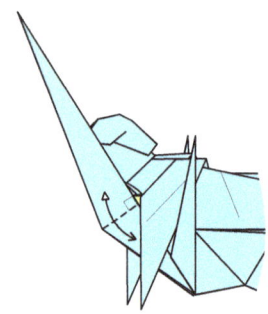

71. Precrease.

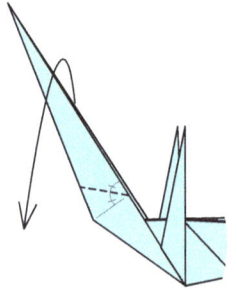

72. Man omitted for clarity. Valley fold, creasing sharply.

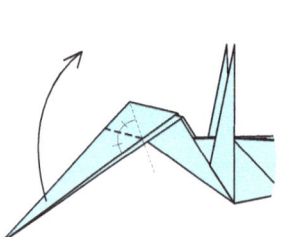

73. Valley fold up, creasing sharply.

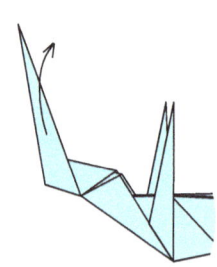

74. Unfold the pleat.

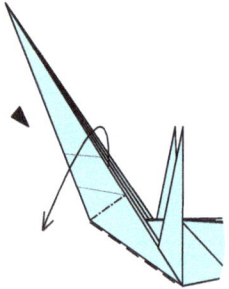

75. Lightly squash fold, leaving one layer at the left and three at the right.

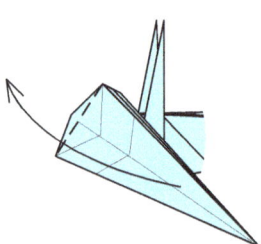

76. Lightly valley fold up.

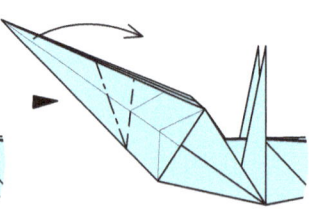

77. Precrease along the angle bisector.

78. Squash fold.

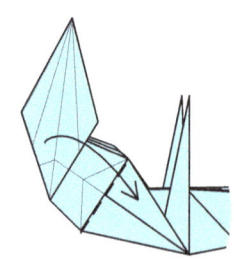

79. Swing back down.

the missionary

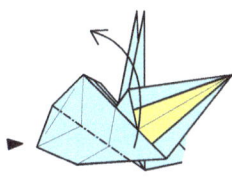

80. Squash upwards.

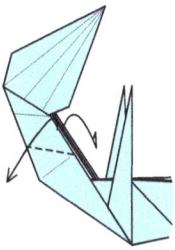

81. Outside reverse fold, distributing only one layer at the forefront.

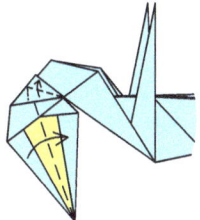

82. Valley fold over while swiveling.

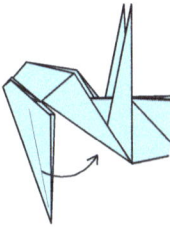

83. Rotate the hair section.

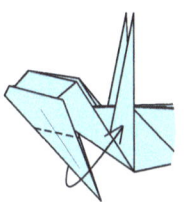

84. Valley fold up the tip.

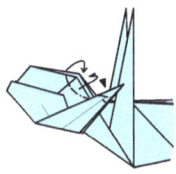

85. Squash fold the tip. Shape the head.

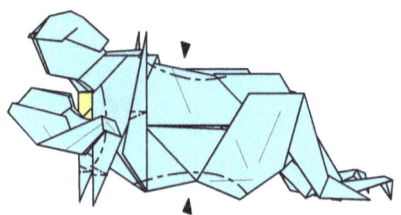

86. Shape and position the arms and bodies to taste.

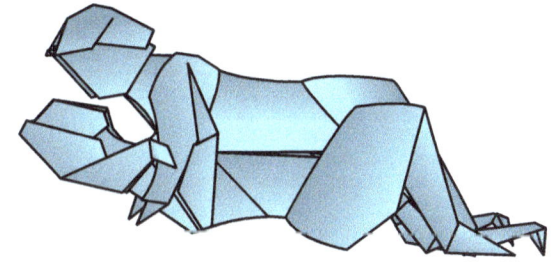

87. Completed *The Missionary*.

It's All Greek To Me

About

The folks from Athens have made tremendous contributions towards medicine, philosophy and athletics, yet the one thing that bears the Greek name is a sexual position. To give credit where credit is due, the Greeks were probably not the originators of rear-entry sex. Many animals have been doing it doggy-style, well before humans were even around. Somehow the Greeks popularized the position, so the *It's All Greek to Me* homage stands. Art replicates life, so naturally the origami version of the couple is joined at the rump. For that matter they are joined along a portion of the legs as well, making for a very efficient structure. Of course, the arms are free, which is the advantage of the Greek position.

Tips

Step forty-five will almost surprisingly fall into place. The key is to form the mountain fold along the top edge of the legs first. The long valley fold should form naturally. The objective of step sixty-six is to conceal as much of the flap as possible. Try to spread squash as much as possible, even at the expense of neatness. Remember that area will be concealed in the following step.

it's all greek to me

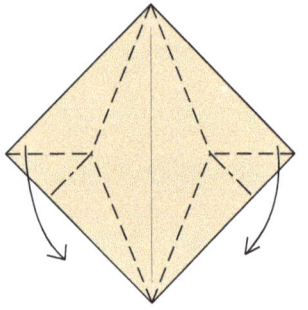

1. Form rabbit ears on both sides.

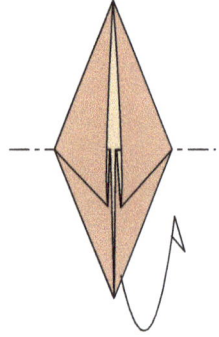

2. Swing the flap back.

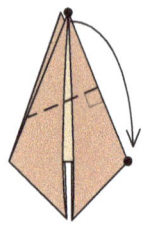

3. Valley fold over to the indicated corner.

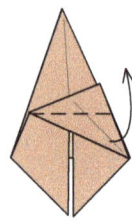

4. Valley fold up.

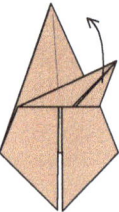

5. Unfold the pleat.

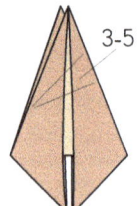

6. Repeat steps 3-5 in mirror image.

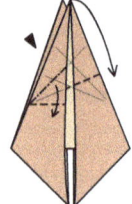

7. Squash fold.

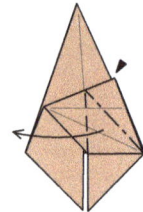

8. Squash again.

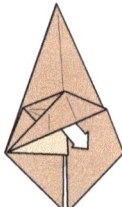

9. Pull out the single layer, and flatten.

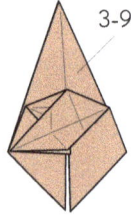

10. Repeat steps 3-9 on the flap behind.

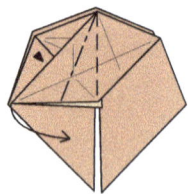

11. Squash the center flap.

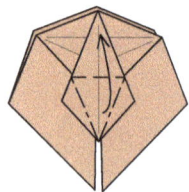

12. Petal fold.

it's all greek to me

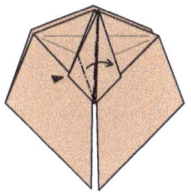
13. Fold over one layer, allowing a spread squash to form.

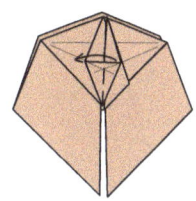
14. Swing one layer back.

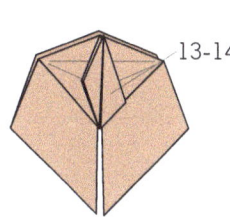
15. Repeat steps 13-14 in mirror image.

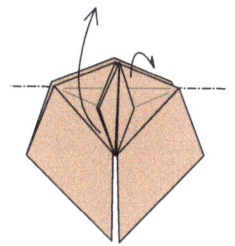
16. Flip the top section.

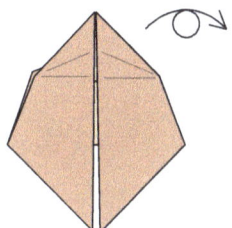
17. Turn over.

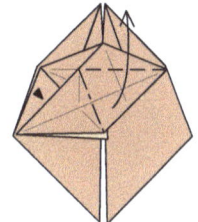
18. Squash fold the top flap.

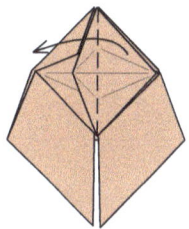
19. Valley fold over.

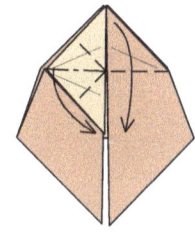
20. Valley fold down, while incorporating a reverse fold.

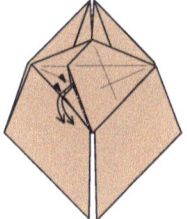
21. Reverse fold the two flaps.

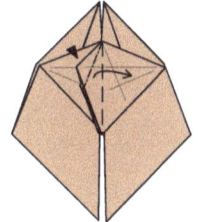
22. Spread squash the center flap.

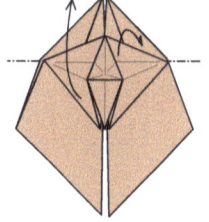
23. Flip the top section.

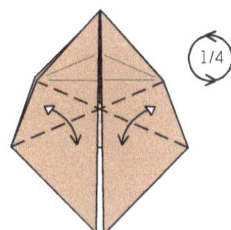
24. Precrease and then rotate the model 1/4 turn.

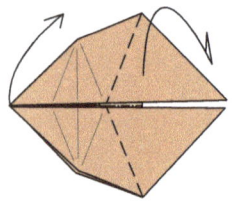

25. Mountain fold the model in half while outside reverse folding the top section along the existing creases.

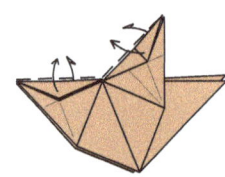

26. Swing the flaps up at each side.

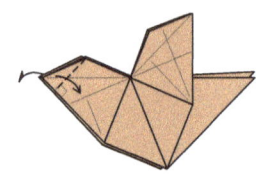

27. Valley fold down at each side.

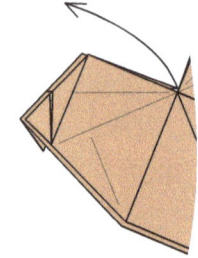

28. Pull up the center flap.

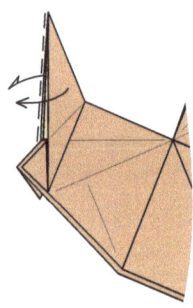

29. Swing the sides forward, releasing the trapped layers.

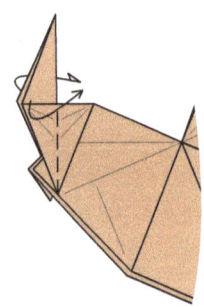

30. Swing the sides back.

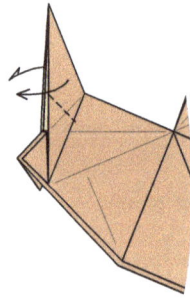

31. Outside reverse fold.

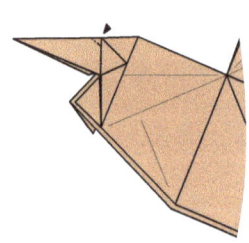

32. Make a tiny sink.

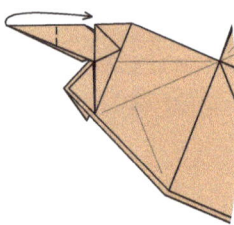

33. Outside reverse fold (a little more than half the flap's length).

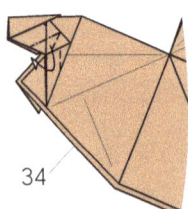

34. Swivel under. Repeat behind.

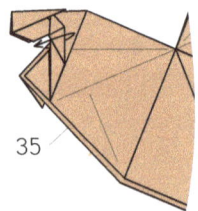

35. Wrap a single layer around to the surface (like a closed sink). Repeat behind.

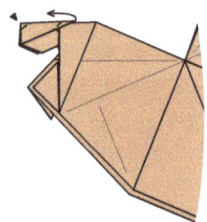

36. Sink the corner, and outside reverse fold the tip.

it's all greek to me

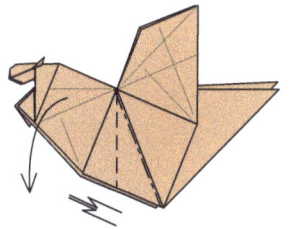

37. Crimp the front section down.

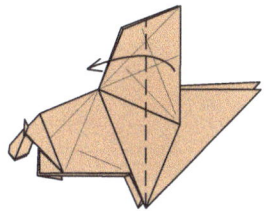

38. Valley fold the top flap.

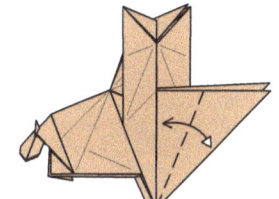

39. Precrease lightly.

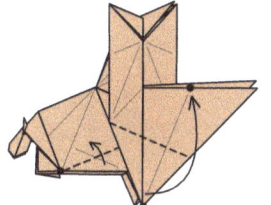

40. Valley fold the corner to the crease, allowing a squash to form.

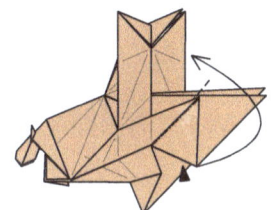

41. Reverse fold the flap.

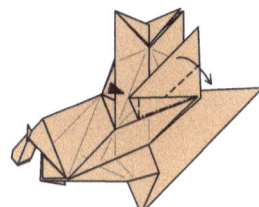

42. Reverse fold the flap back down.

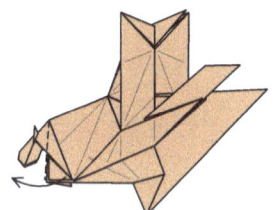

43. Swing over the flap.

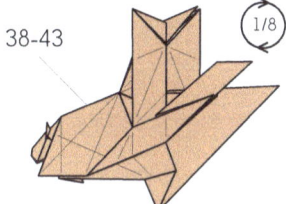

44. Repeat steps 38-43 behind. Rotate the model 1/8th of a turn.

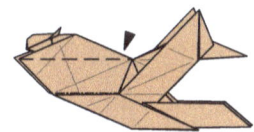

45. Closed reverse fold. The valley fold should form naturally.

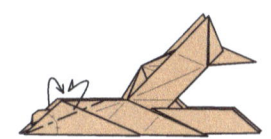

46. Mountain fold the outer edges in along the angle bisectors.

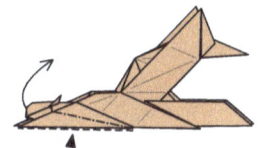

47. Slide the center flap upwards, allowing a mountain fold to form along the angle bisector.

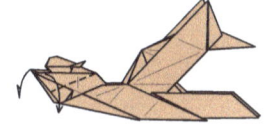

48. Swing the side flaps down.

85

it's all greek to me

49. Swivel fold the arms at each side.

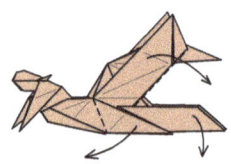

50. Unfold the top pleats.

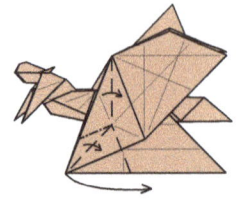

51. Valley fold the bottom flap, while swiveling over the top layer.

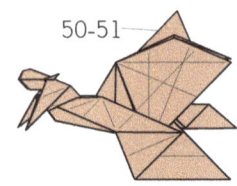

52. Repeat steps 50-51 behind.

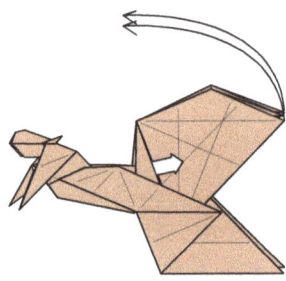

53. Pull up, while releasing the trapped layers at each side.

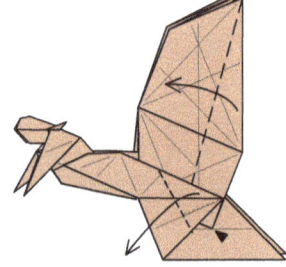

54. Valley fold the side, while swivel folding the point downwards.

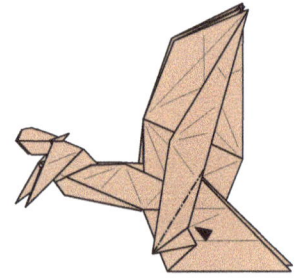

55. Sink along the existing crease.

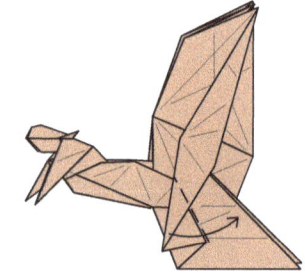

56. Swing the flap over.

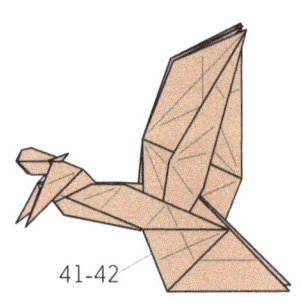

57. Replace the folds from steps 41-42.

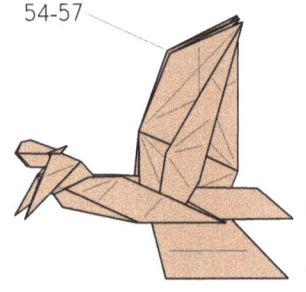

58. Repeat steps 54-57 behind.

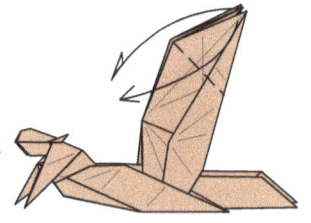

59. Swing the two side flaps down.

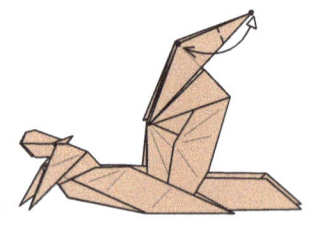

60. Precrease the flap.

it's all greek to me

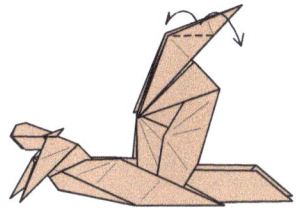
61. Outside reverse fold, using the last crease as a guide.

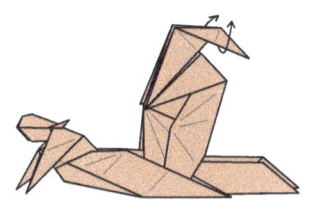
62. Wrap around a layer at each side.

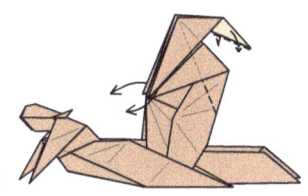
63. Pull the side flaps forward, allowing the sides of the top flap to come down.

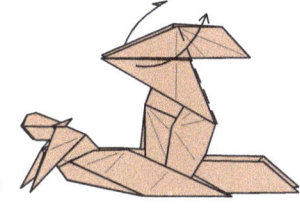
64. Swing the side flaps up.

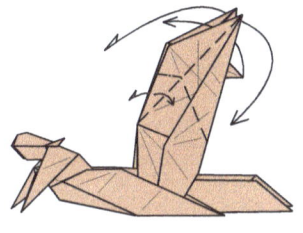
65. Bring the flaps back down again, while crimping the center flap.

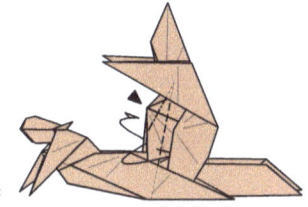
66. Spread squash the center flap, tucking the resulting flaps into the side pockets.

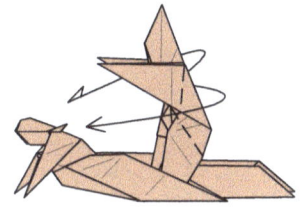
67. Outside reverse fold.

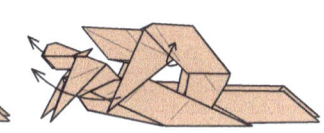
68. Pull out the two side crimps.

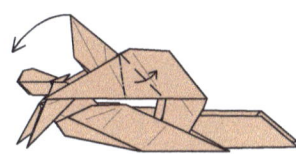
69. Replace the two side crimps, changing the direction of the folds.

70. Mountain fold.

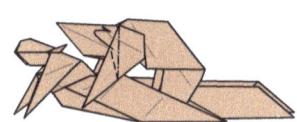
71. Pleat the arm flap.

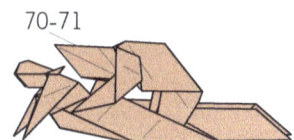
72. Repeat steps 70-71 behind.

87

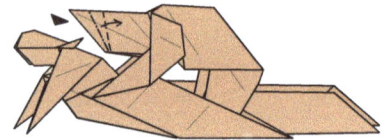
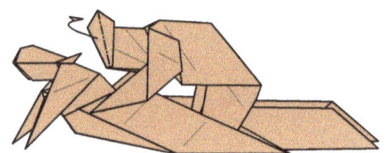
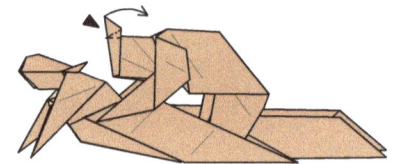

73. Spread squash.

74. Mountain fold.

75. Squash and wrap the tip around the head.

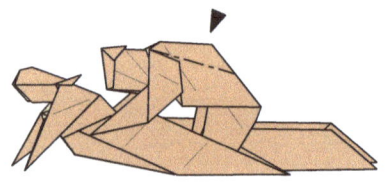
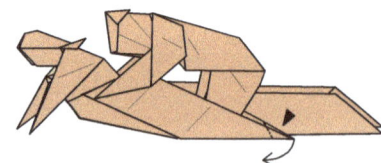
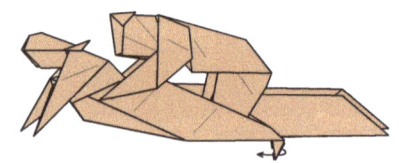

76. Sink the top edge (similar to a spread squash).

77. Reverse fold.

78. Open out the flap.

it's all greek to me

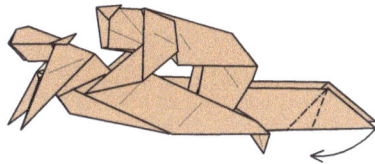

79. Pleat the flap down.

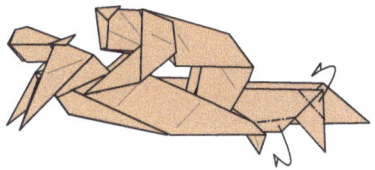

80. Shape with mountain folds.

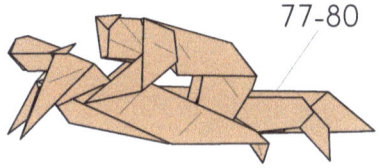

81. Repeat steps 77-80 behind.

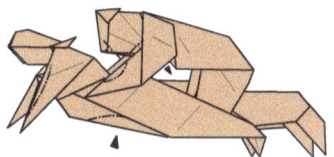

82. Shape the head with mountain folds and round the model to taste.

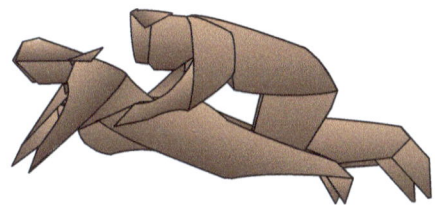

83. Completed *It's All Greek to Me*.

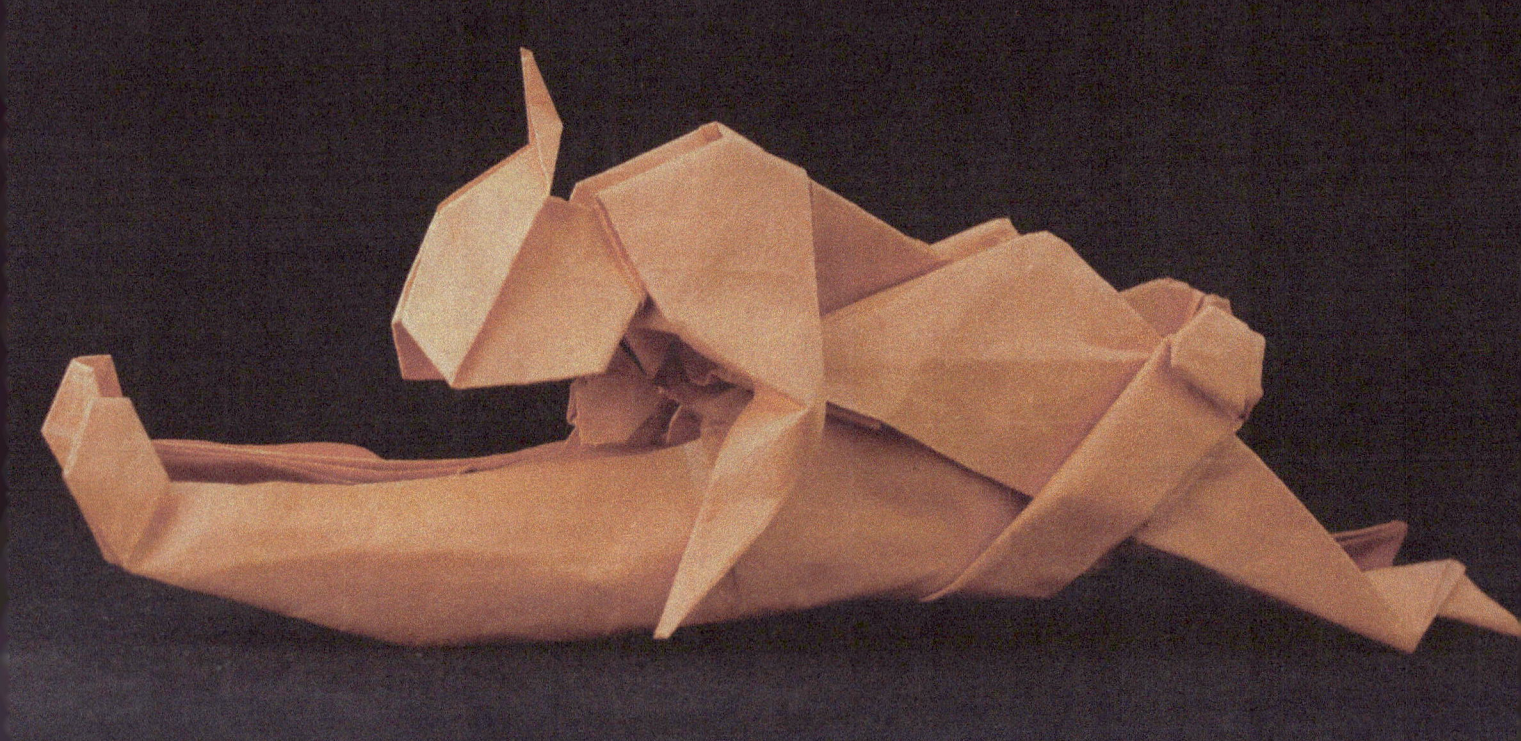

Each One Eat One

About

Origami master Robert Neale came up with a colorful name for his multi-piece interlocking paper creation. Little did he know how well *Each One Eat One* would apply to the most equitable of sexual positions. Some body contortions are necessary to get the sixty-nine position to work, unless you are one of the lucky few to find a perfectly mated partner. A bit of paper acrobatics was necessary to get the origami version to work as well. For instance, the woman's legs and buttocks originate from different areas, and the man's arms conceal the would-be seam. The penis is generously well endowed however, so the woman does not have to contort as much to reach it. If only we could be so flexible in real life.

Tips

The arms on the man become very thick, so exercise care when performing any related folds from steps seventy-five onwards. This very thickness conceals the tapering folds in step seventy-six to shape the woman's legs. Be sure to adjust these folds to follow the taper of the buttocks. Curved folds are shown in step eighty-three to position the legs. For more extreme positioning, you can also try harder-edged crimp folds.

— each one eat one —

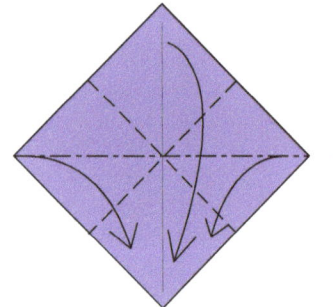

1. Collapse downwards.

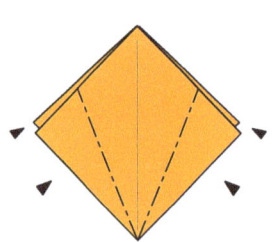

2. Reverse fold the four corners.

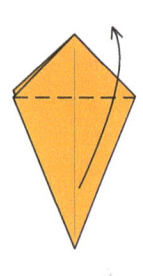

3. Valley fold the front flap up.

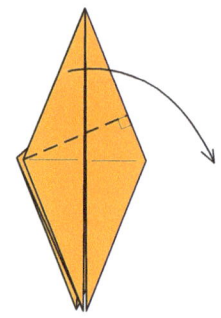

4. Valley fold over.

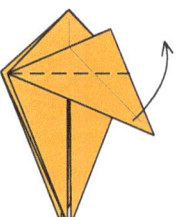

5. Valley fold back up.

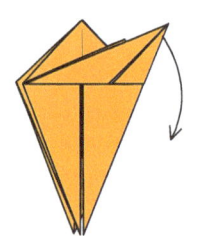

6. Unfold the pleat.

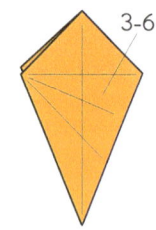

7. Repeat steps 3-6 in mirror image.

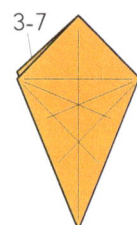

8. Repeat steps 3-7 behind.

each one eat one

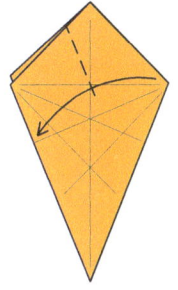

9. Bring the corner to the crease, folding only at the top.

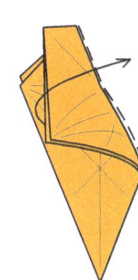

10. Unfold.

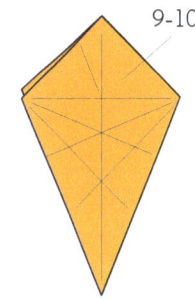

11. Repeat steps 9-10 in mirror image.

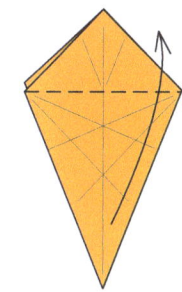

12. Valley fold up.

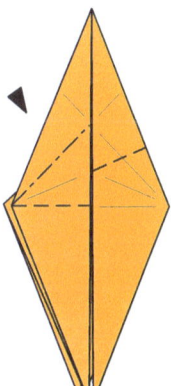

13. Form an asymmetrical squash fold.

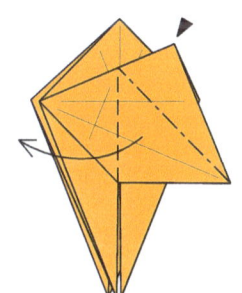

14. Squash again.

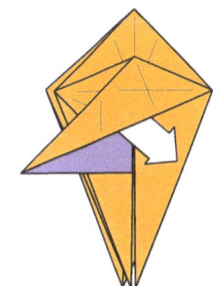

15. Pull out the single layer.

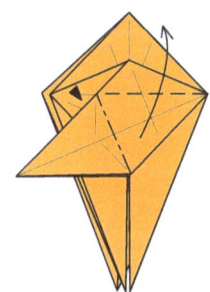

16. Squash fold.

— each one eat one —

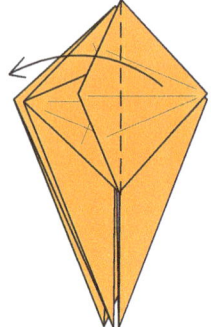

17. Valley fold over.

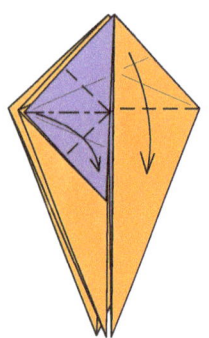

18. Valley fold down while incorporating a reverse fold.

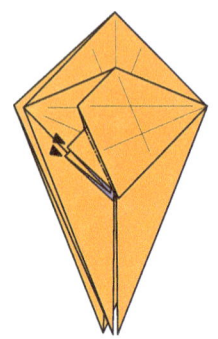

19. Reverse fold the two corners.

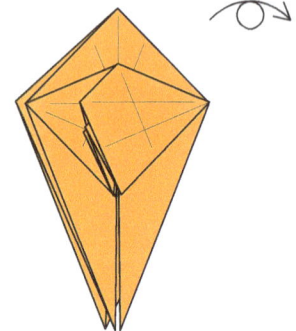

20. Turn over.

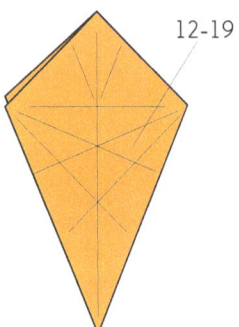

21. Repeat steps 12-19.

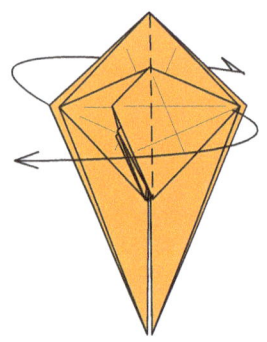

22. Swing over a large flap, front and back.

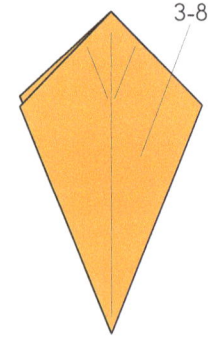

23. Repeat steps 3-8.

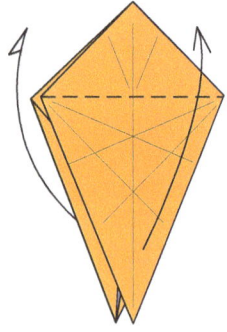

24. Valley fold the large flaps up.

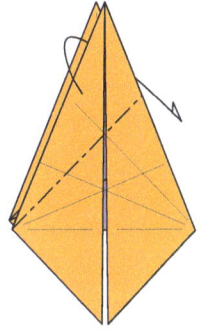

25. Mountain fold along the existing crease.

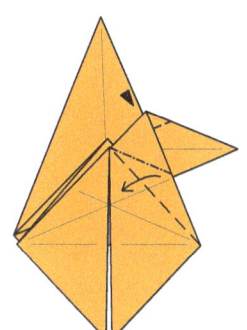

26. Swivel fold.

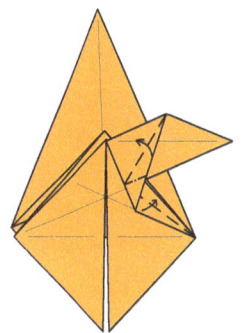

27. Swivel again.

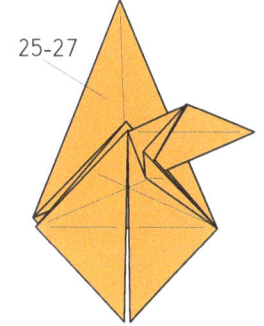

28. Repeat steps 25-27 behind (and in mirror image).

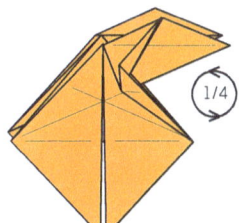

29. Rotate the model.

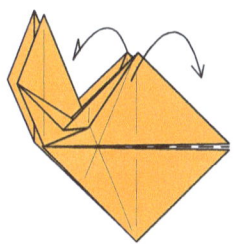

30. Swing the large flaps down.

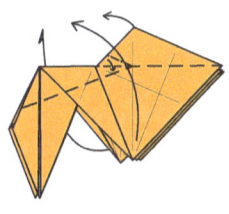

31. Outside reverse fold the large flaps, allowing a pleat to form. Do not crease sharply. Use the existing creases as a guide.

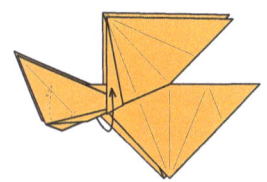

32. Wrap a layer around to the surface. Repeat behind.

each one eat one

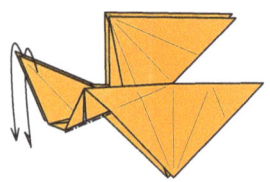

33. Swing the flaps down and flatten the model.

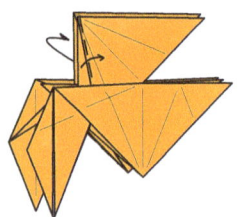

34. Swivel the flap over. Repeat behind.

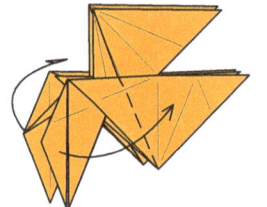

35. Lightly swing the flaps over.

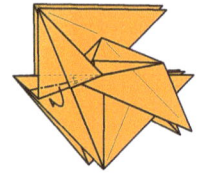

36. Lightly mountain fold along the angle bisector.

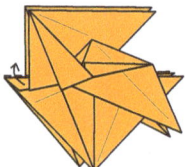

37. Swing the layer up and flatten.

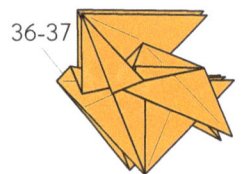

38. Repeat steps 36-37 behind.

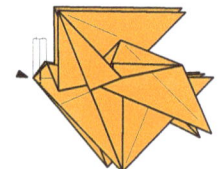

39. Closed sink the tip (a triangular or open sink is okay if it is too difficult).

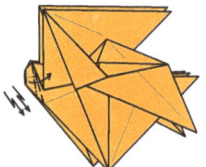

40. Crimp over to the folded edge.

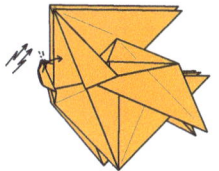

41. Form a tiny crimp at the top. The paper will buckle slightly.

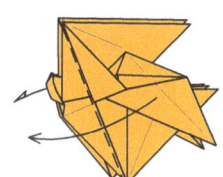

42. Swing the two flaps back over.

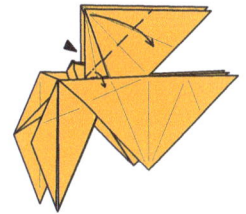

43. Squash fold.

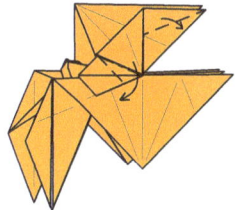

44. Swivel fold. Do not flatten.

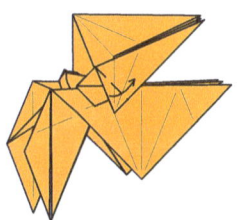

45. Valley fold up and flatten.

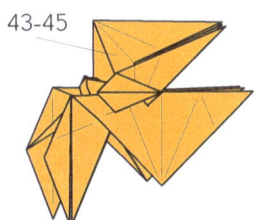

46. Repeat steps 43-45 behind.

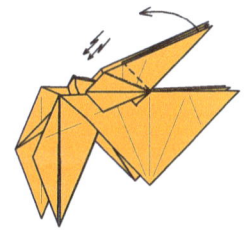

47. Crimp upwards.

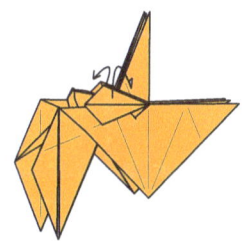

48. Wrap a single layer around. Repeat behind.

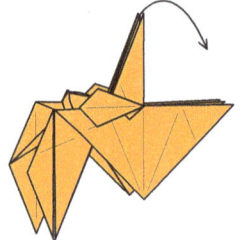
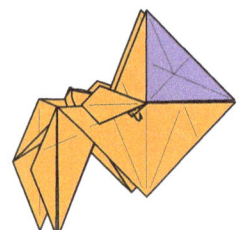
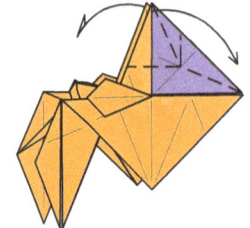
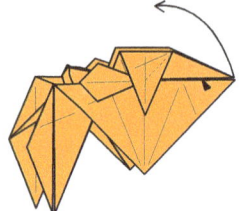

49. Pull down the center flap, allowing it to come undone.

50. Mountain fold the protruding flap. Repeat behind.

51. Collapse the flaps down, using the existing creases as a guide.

52. Reverse fold upwards.

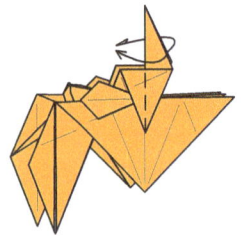

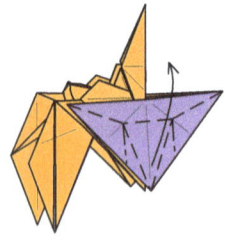

53. Swing both flaps towards the left.

54. Swing the top flap over, allowing the center flap to come undone.

55. Collapse the flap upwards.

56. Swing the flap back over.

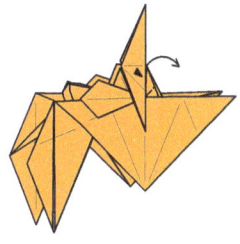

57. Squash fold the tiny flap.

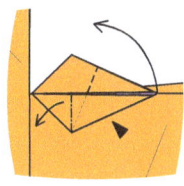

58. Detail of flap. Form an asymmetrical squash.

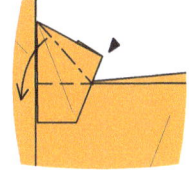

59. Squash fold again.

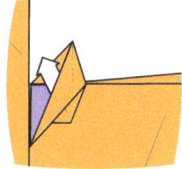

60. Pull out the single layer.

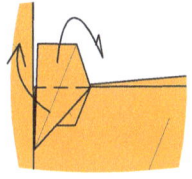

61. Swing one flap up, and the other one down.

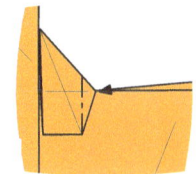

62. Sink the corner.

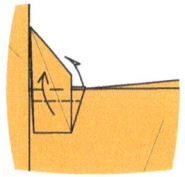

63. Pleat both sides upwards (see the next step for approximate positioning).

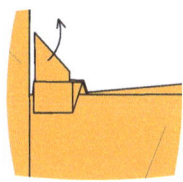

64. Stretch upwards (allowing the center to collapse naturally).

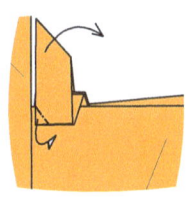

65. Mountain fold the corner. Repeat behind. Pull the flap forward.

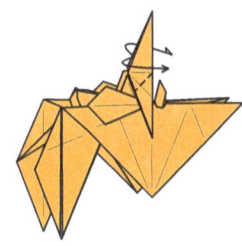

66. Outside reverse fold.

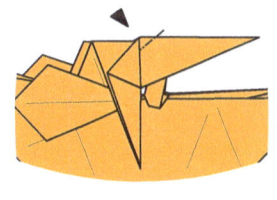

67. Make a tiny sink.

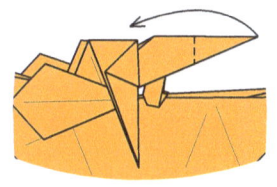

68. Outside reverse fold (a little more than half the flap's length).

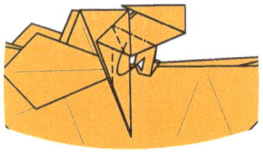

69. Swivel under, and repeat behind. This is a significant step for this model.

70. Wrap a single layer around to the surface (like a closed sink).

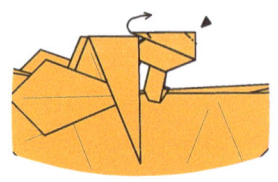

71. Sink the corner, and outside reverse fold the tip.

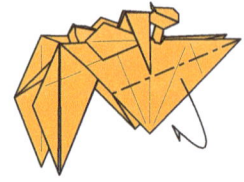

72. Mountain fold the large flap.

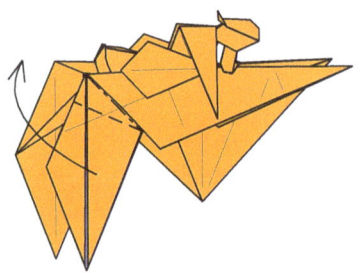

73. Pleat the flap upwards.

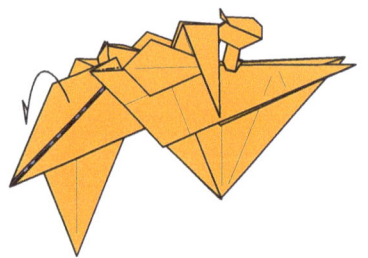

74. Mountain fold the flap, allowing a squash to form behind.

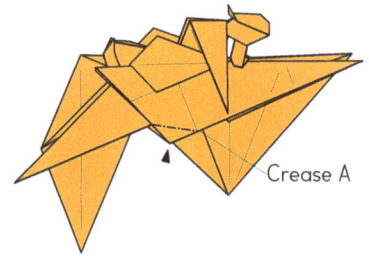

75. Form a tiny reverse fold. Note how it hits the flap and crease A.

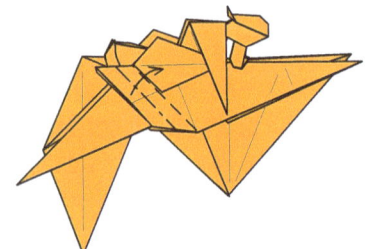

75. Pleat the entire flap forward.

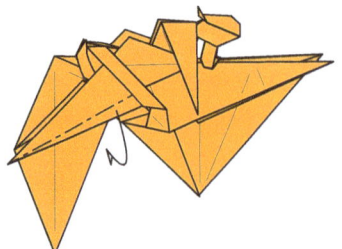

76. Adjust the taper of the flap with a mountain fold.

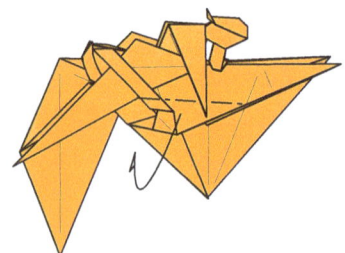

77. Mountain fold the lower edge into the model. Note where the fold hits the crease.

each one eat one

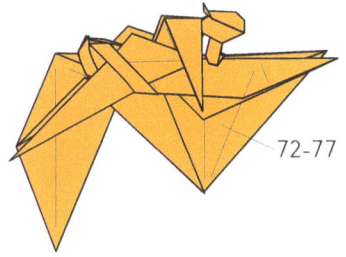

78. Repeat steps 72-77 behind.

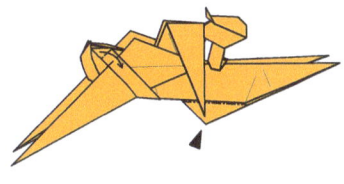

79. Sink the protruding point. Pleat the hands.

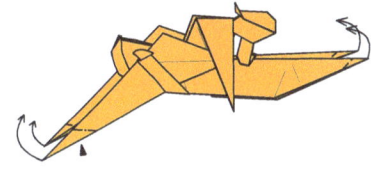

80. Outside reverse fold at the right and squash upwards at the left of the model.

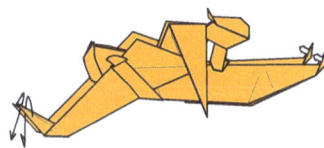

81. Pull out paper at the right, and mountain fold at the left of the model.

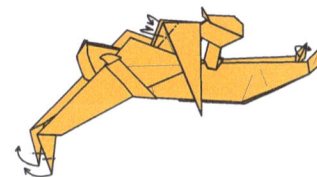

82. Unsink at the right and reverse fold at the left of the model. Mountain fold the shoulders.

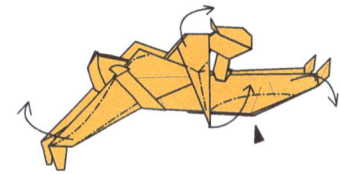

83. Rabbit ear the arms, pull the woman's torso forward slightly, and shape the model to taste.

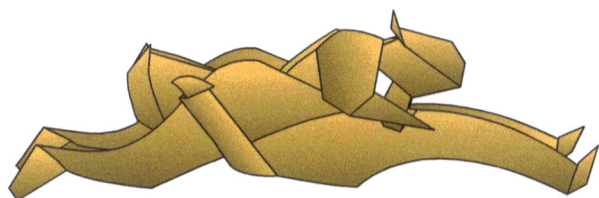

84. Completed *Each One Eat One*.

Materials and Methods

In theory, the only things required for origami is a piece of paper and a pair of hands. In practice, however, you will want to have the right materials for the project at hand. For initial practice attempts, you will want to use papers that are easy to fold, but not necessarily of presentable quality. The two most popular practice papers are commercial origami paper (sometimes sold as kami) and American foil. Both of these papers are available colored on one side, and white on the other. I much prefer using American foil as it holds its shape more easily. These papers feature a thin layer of decorative foil that helps your model hold its shape. Most of the origami supply houses sell a 10" version as their largest size, but some thinner wrapping paper can be used if you are looking for something larger. Japanese foil is thinner, and generally easier to fold than the American variety, albeit more expensive. Kami is better for those who have trouble with reverse folds and sinks. Both types of papers will yield adequate results, but almost invariably, more decorative choices will make your models look better.

For display-worthy efforts, you will want to use papers and methods that heighten the final result, possibly at the expense of ease of folding. Such methods include foil-backing and wet folding, which includes the related technique of back coating. Both approaches allow the paper-folding artist to use material combinations to create interesting effects.

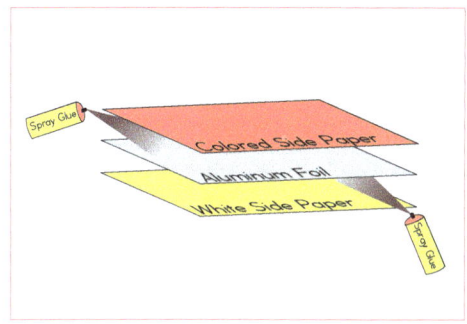

Foil Backing

Foil backing is a great way to utilize nonporous materials, and papers with patterns that could get ruined with water (such as newsprint). Foil backing is the process of adding a layer of aluminum foil (yes, the same material you can find at virtually any grocery store) to paper, to give the resulting material unique folding characteristics. A common backing choice is tissue paper, which further enhances the folding properties of the foil (this combination is also known as "tissue foil"). Regardless of the backing material, the metal-like quality allows folds to instantly stay where they are placed. Spray adhesive is used to bond the layers together. This is also known as artist's adhesive or photo mounting spray, and it contains the same glue found on adhesive tape. You can find this at most art supply stores, but you will find it much cheaper at a hardware or office supply store. While 3M's Spray Mount is usually ideal, some projects (typically involving very thick papers) will require something like 3M's Super77 Spray Adhesive. All work should be done in a well-ventilated area, as the glue is toxic. You will also want to protect your floor with newspaper. Place a sheet of foil on the floor. Leave the shinier side up first, and use as the surface for the main color. In most cases, the foil will be the limiting factor as far as size is concerned, so use as large a sheet as necessary. Spray the glue onto the surface of the foil according to the manufacturer's directions. If you have a choice of nozzles, use the one with a finer mist. When spraying, be sure to cover the entire surface area of the foil, while paying special attention to the edges. After spraying, you should give the glue about a minute to get tacky.

The next step is to apply your paper to the tacky surface. Start by adhering the bottom edge of your paper to the bottom edge of the foil. Then start working your way upwards until the foil is completely covered. You can also use a baker's rolling pin to apply the paper. Another variation is to start at one corner and work your way to the opposite corner. Try several methods to see which feels most comfortable. For thicker papers, it might be easier to simply drop the paper onto the foil. When you are done, rub out any wrinkles, and then apply another layer of paper on the other side.

To get the largest possible square, cut along the edge of the foil, which should be visible through the layers of paper, provided your papers are translucent enough. If you wish you can also tear through the foil, which is surprisingly accurate (and fun), provided you are using thin enough paper. First, score the paper, unfold, and turn over to leave the resulting crease in mountain fold formation. The paper can easily be torn in this position. Of course you won't get the largest possible square this way, but it is easier to be accurate.

Using a rotary cutting board is ideal when tearing is not possible, or you cannot see the silhouette of the foil through your backing paper. While a traditional guillotine cutter might suffice, spending an extra $100 or so on a rotary cutter is worth the investment for the serious paperfolding artist. These can be purchased at better art supply stores or photography supply stores. A pair of scissors can be used when a paper cutter is not as convenient.

f you wish to make a square that is wider than your piece of foil, there is a way to accomplish this. First, you have to adhere two (or more) strips of foil together. If you spray along the edge of one piece and attach the other piece along that edge, the results are remarkably seamless. Most likely, the paper you will want to use on the surface will be smaller than the foil piece you have prepared. There is a way around this hurdle as well. First, you should fold your foil in half. The resulting surface area should now be small enough for your paper. Before you use any adhesive, place a sheet of newspaper between the fold to avoid getting any glue on the inner layers. You can now adhere your papers on each side of the foil. When you are done with the gluing part, use a scissor to cut along the folded edge. After you unfold your piece, rub out the crease, and the seam will almost disappear. You can repeat the same process for the other side.

When folding larger models (having a giant paper penis is a great artistic effect), you might find certain portions to be flimsy. While some people use wire to add rigidity, stuffing layers of foil often works even better. You can fold a piece of foil over upon itself a few times to make it many layers thick. This can be placed between the layers of the parts of the model that need more rigidity.

If you are using tissue as the backing paper, where the properties of the foil are at their most extreme, you are in for a radically different folding experience. By themselves, foil and tissue make for flimsy and weak folding materials, but together you have one of the strongest and most resilient materials around. Also, when you make a crease, it will hold very well. It will hold so well that it is difficult to change its direction (i.e., valley to mountain). This makes procedures that require precreasing, such as sinks, difficult to perform. You can unfold the paper after precreasing, rub out the creases that have to be changed, and replace them with new folds that are in the right direction. Unlike commercial foil paper, you can rub out unwanted creases without leaving a trace.

While it is true that foil backing will make folding your model more difficult for most if its stages, its properties are fortuitous at the end of a model's folding sequence. If your model has many layers, it can easily be flattened. In extreme cases, a hammer can work wonders. After your model is as flat as you desire, you can shape and pose it any way you wish. Your model will hold that shape forever, until you decide to reshape it, or someone or something inadvertently reshapes it. The latter scenario is obviously undesirable. If you use a slightly thicker paper (such as the aforementioned Japanese papers), you will lose some of the malleability, but will have a much more solid looking model, due to its increased thickness. It can still be bent out of shape, so you should handle such models with care.

Wet Folding

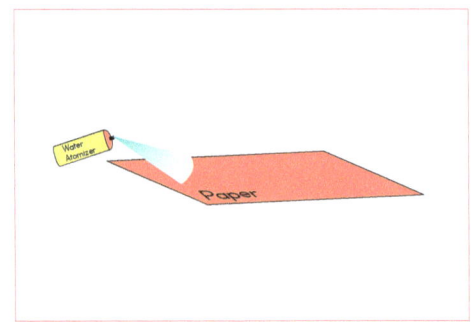

After the above discussion, you might be surprised to discover that few of the pieces photographed for this book employed foil backing techniques. Foil backed paper looks great in person, but the camera lens often picks up the foil through the backing, even when the backing paper seems to be dense enough. Some people like this glowing effect, but for photographs wet folding techniques ensure your paper looks like paper.. The process might be slower, but the results are more permanent.

Wet folding involves lightly dampening your paper during the folding process, so when it finally dries it will retain its shape. When paper is wet, the sizing (glue-like substance) that holds the paper fibers together is loosened. Once the paper is dry again, the sizing will hold the paper in its new position. Taking advantage of this property of paper enables the folder to hold shapes that seem to defy gravity. Not all papers contain a lot of sizing, so you might have to add a methylcellulose paste to your paper before folding. To do this, you first add two tablespoons of methylcellulose powder (which is sold at many art supply stores) to a half cup of boiling water, and mix the compound until it is syrupy. Then add one cup of very cold water and mix again. After about fifteen minutes your paste should be at the right consistency. This paste can now be brushed onto your paper with a standard painter's brush. After the paper is dry, it will be even easier to wet fold. To speed up the drying process, you can use a table fan.

When wet folding it is important to realize your paper will expand, often unevenly. This makes accurate folding much more difficult. Also, reference fold crease lines become difficult to see while paper is wet. For these reasons, you may prefer to delay wetting the paper until key folds are in place. When you are ready to wet the paper, it is important not to allow the paper to get soggy. By using an atomizer's mist sparingly, a leathery texture can be obtained from the paper. These spray bottles can be found at many perfume sections; try to find one with as fine a mist as possible.

Holding your model in position while drying can be a creative challenge. Tools that work well include twist ties (the plastic coated ones that are often used for electrical wire packing), portable clamps, and painter's masking tape. As an example, you can wind a twist tie around the appendages your model, bend them into the desired position, and secure them to a flat surface with masking tape (this is how origami artists perform paper bondage). After further moistening your model with your atomizer, it will retain its stance after it is dry and your bindings have been removed.

Back Coating

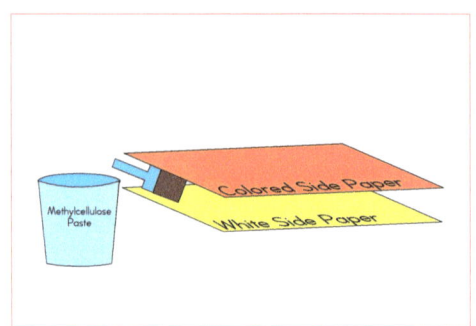

A related technique to wet folding is back coating. Since most specialty papers are monochromatic, the two-toned effect in many origami models is lost. You can use methylcellulose paste to adhere two complementing colors of paper together. Brush the paste on one paper, being sure to work on a smooth surface, as the paper will pick up any texture from your working surface. Apply the second sheet on top, brushing it into place. You can cut your square once it is dry, using a table fan to expedite the process. Again, a rotary cutter is recommended. The materials you chose to mate together should both be porous and fibrous enough to stay together, otherwise you might have to resort to foil backing.

Papers that have worked well include the Unryu variety (both regular and soft) from both Japan and Thailand. These papers might be labeled as containing mulberry or kozo fiber, but other fibers will work as well. Yatsuo papers from Japan, which are made from kozo and sulphite pulp, have a much smoother look than the Unryu papers. These and other fine art papers can be found at better art stores and via mail order (see the Sources section at the end of this book for details). You can expect to pay about three to four dollars for a 25" x 37" sheet.

Other important paper considerations include weight, which is how a material's thickness is described. To give you a gauge of what this means, standard copy paper is often at 20 Gr/M2 weight. Of course, you will double your thickness if you are bonding two sheets together. You should not let paper thickness scare you, as moistening your sheet with an atomizer will make it much more pliable. When dealing with lighter colors, you might have to work with thicker papers just to get the right opacity (but you can mate them with lighter weight darker papers if you are trying to avoid additional thickness). As a test, you can hold the paper against a black surface to see how well it eclipses its backing. Sometimes, having the contrasting color show through is a good thing, as your color choices will seem to blend a bit. One thing you would like to avoid is having your paper bleed (having the dye run) when wet. The most temperamental colors tend to be reds and black, but it is a good idea to test out a sheet first if possible. With enough experimentation, you should be able to conceive the perfect material for any model.

Ratio Information

Anally Receptive 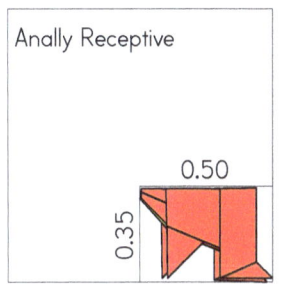 0.50 / 0.35	**Ankh** 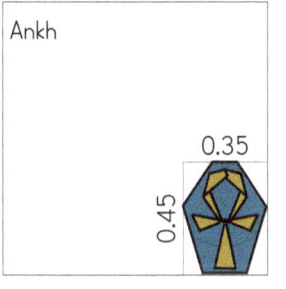 0.35 / 0.45	**Smoker** 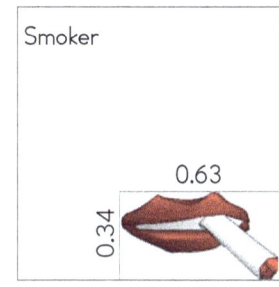 0.63 / 0.34	**Lips Together, Teeth Apart** 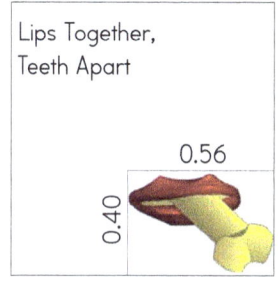 0.56 / 0.40
Mouney Fold 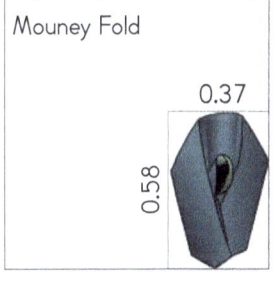 0.37 / 0.58	**Prince Albert** 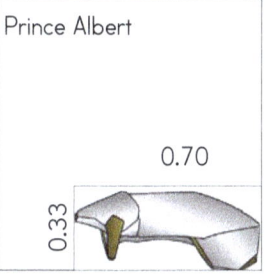 0.70 / 0.33	**Randy Rabbit** 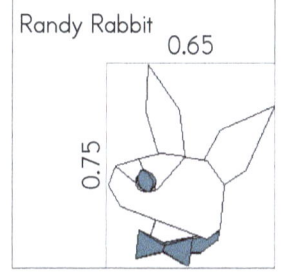 0.65 / 0.75	**Taking a Hand in Female Matters** 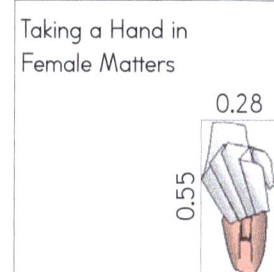 0.28 / 0.55
Taking a Hand in Male Matters 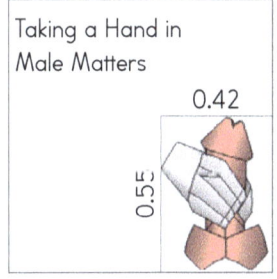 0.42 / 0.55	**The Missionary** 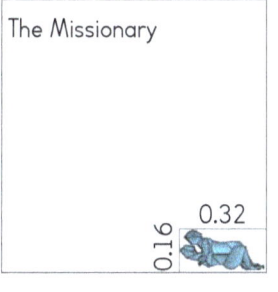 0.32 / 0.16	**It's All Greek to Me**  0.47 / 0.23	**Each One Eat One** 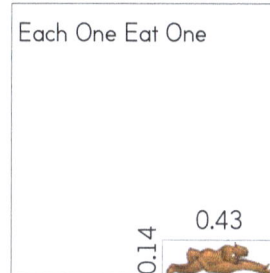 0.43 / 0.14

www.ingramcontent.com/pod-product-compliance
Lightning Source LLC
Chambersburg PA
CBHW051348110526
44591CB00025B/2939